Sammarinesi in Michigan and Beyond

Russell M. Magnaghi

Sammarinesi in Michigan and Beyond

ISBN: 978-1-257-77283-4
Imprint: Lulu.com

Book design by James Shefchik.

Dedicated to
Livio Capicchioni
&
Joseph Putti

Table of Contents

Introduction

Millions of immigrants have come to the shores of the United States to make their homes and better lives through opportunity. Of these millions who came were the Sammarinesi, a small ethnic group that is little known, who are people usually associated with Italians. Newspaper articles throughout the twentieth century provided limited coverage about the Republic and its history; many short "did you know" stories were common. In reality, coming from a microstate, the Sammarinesi are found across the globe: from farmers in Argentina, to factory workers in France, miners in Belgium to social workers in Africa. Metro Detroit is home to the largest number of Sammarinesi in the United States, with smaller numbers found in the Greater New York area and Sandusky, Ohio. Smaller numbers of immigrants are found from Cleveland, Ohio to Birmingham, Alabama and westward to Montana and California.

It is essential to tell their story for a few reasons. They are a relatively tiny ethnic minority, unfortunately commonly merged with Italians. Furthermore, little has been written about them in English due to these disadvantages. So this narrative takes on the responsibility of telling the story of the Sammarinesi in the United States. The approach focuses on numerous individual stories, due to the fact that Sammarinesi and Sammarinese-Americans in southeast Michigan and neighboring Ohio, through their generosity of time, provided their memories in oral interviews, which are key to the story. Newspaper articles, census data and immigration records added to the story across the United States. The final critical ingredient to telling this story is the fact that these people retain an unbelievably strong attachment to their homeland, where citizenship is maintained, and every effort is taken to preserve their heritage. So the story can proceed.

Acknowledgements

While researching the book *Italians in Michigan*, I met Livio Capicchioni in the evening of August 16, 2000, and said that I planned to, at least briefly, mention the Sammarinesi in the book. He quickly and fortunately set me straight about these unique people and said: "They have a separate and matchless history and heritage, which is not to be lost among Italians."

So a new research project was begun. Historical narratives are based on documents from libraries, archives and oral interviews with individuals. The first obstacle was the fact that there were few published sources available on Detroit's Sammarinese community. Then I met Joseph Putti, the Sammarinese Midwest consul, a kind, friendly, and thoughtful individual who stressed his complete and unwavering interest in the project. Realizing that there are so few sources, he closely worked with me to identify individuals to be interviewed and share their stories of their immigrant experience. Over a period of time he organized the process and individuals who conveniently met with me at his office. If Livio awakened me to conduct the study, Joseph provided me with sources of information. It was an absolute pleasure to work with Joseph who so loved his rich heritage.

The third individual who helped this project was Roberto Balsimelli, Sammarinese consul general in New York. He readily assisted me with the New York portion of the story. His assistance has allowed me to bring the three points of Sammarinese settlement together.

Between 2002 and 2004 with the aid of Joseph Putti, I was put in contact with a host of people who provided me with valuable information about the Sammarinese immigrant experience. The following people provided me with their memories – Arthur Amati, Walter and Dolores Babboni, Gabriele Bugli, Paul Calmi, Lucio Capicchioni, Fernando Casali, Dino Crescentini, Nazarina Bolini Crooks, Giancarlo Ferri, Lisette Gatti, Dennis Giannini, Cafiero and Regina Manzarolli, Anthony Muscioni, Frank and Diane Paoletti, Joseph Putti, Giuseppe Selva, Gloriana Casadei Severini, Lina Bizzocchi Uberti, and Secondo and Pierene Zanotti. All these interviews are deposited at the Bentley Library, University of Michigan, Ann Arbor. Many of these individuals also provided me with personal documentation, photographs and books. Without these individuals this publication would not exist.

I must add that in recent years electronic resources on-line – newspapers.com and ancestry.com – these resources have been extremely useful for tracking individuals and their enigmatic history and lives. Federal census data and naturalization and immigration records also aided me.

As one studies the Sammarinese ethnic heritage it becomes apparent that there are missing records. In order to create a full narrative it was important to visit the sites – history-on-the-hoof – where the story unfolded in order to better understand the history. This story was enhanced by visits to little known sites as Kelleys Island, Ohio; West 10th

Street in New York City's Greenwich Village; Queens and Astoria, New York; Oakwood-Fort neighborhood and other sites throughout Metro Detroit, Michigan.

The work has been edited and revised by a loyal and experienced staff – Ted Bays, Lore Ann Parent, and James F. Shefchik. However, in the end I take credit for the work and apologize in advance for any errors or missing data.

Land, People & History

The term "Sammarinese" brings forth questions in people's minds when first heard: What? Who? This is the official title of the people from the Republic of San Marino, but it offers little help to the bewildered. So where and what is the Republic of San Marino?

It is officially known as The Most Serene Republic of San Marino (*Serenissima Repubblica di San Marino*) and is located in the Apennine Mountains, nine miles southwest of the city of Rimini, on the north central coast of Italy within view of the Adriatic Sea. This enclave is completely surrounded by Italy with Emilia-Romagna to the north and the Marches-Urbino to the west and south. The tiny nation is a mere 24 square miles shaped in an irregular rectangular form with a maximum length of eight miles. This is smaller than an American township, which measures 36 square miles. San Marino is the third-smallest country in Europe, with only Monaco (499 acres) and Vatican City (109 acres) being smaller.[1]

The tiny territory consists of rugged mountainous terrain dominated by Mt. Titano, 2,457 feet above sea level, where the capital, the City of San Marino (2020– 4,500 pop.) is located, surrounded by triple walls. The territory is crossed by the Ausa, San Marino, Fiumicello, and Marano Rivers, which flow into the Adriatic Sea. The arable land amounts to 16.67 percent of the total and the natural resource is building stone. The climate is Mediterranean with warm summers and mild winters. It is obvious that these rather negative land factors are a main force, driving the citizens to seek economic opportunity outside of the Republic.

The population of the Republic in 2020 was 33,958 with 4,800 foreign residents, mostly Italian. There are another 12,000 Sammarinesi living abroad: 5,700 in Italy, 3,000 in the United States, 1,900 in France and 1,600 in Argentina. The principal ethnic majority is the Sammarinese who are a mixture of Mediterranean, Alpine, Adriatic, and Nordic ethnic stocks and account for 84 percent of the population.

Given the small size of the nation the population density is high at 971 persons per square mile. The urban population is 97.1 percent: Serraville (9,258 pop.), Borgo Maggione (6,424 pop.), San Marino (4,500 pop.), Domagnano (3,161 pop.), Fiorentino (2,510 pop.), and Acquaviva (1,530 pop.).

History

San Marino is the only surviving Italian microstate and claims to be the world's oldest surviving republic. According to legend San Marino was begun when a Christian stonecutter known only by the single name, Marinus (literally from "from the sea") later venerated as St. Marinus, emigrated in 297 A.D. from the Croatian island of Rab across the Adriatic Sea. He built a chapel and dwelling on Mount Titano and lived as a hermit. Later a monastery was added, land donated; and Christians fleeing persecution by Emperor Diocletian found a new home. 301 A.D. is considered the foundation date of San Marino.

By the ninth century documents show that there was a well-organized, open, and proud community governed by a bishop. Prior to 1243 the government was carried out by an assembly of the heads of families known as the Arengo. Change came in that year when the position of captains regent was established to be joint heads of state. The earliest statutes date back to 1263.

Until 1463 San Marino consisted only of Mount Titano. Then due to San Marino joining an alliance against Sigismondo Malatesta, Duke of Rimini, Pope Pius II gave San Marino more land, and its territory from that time are the limits of modern San Marino. Given its small size, neighboring lords found it convenient to seize control over the territory and some were met with civil disobedience. Finally a treaty of protection was signed in 1602 by Pope Clement VIII and went into force in 1631.

The next critical time was the era of the Napoleonic Wars in the late 1790s when the people feared Napoleon would dissolve the republic and incorporate it into the emerging Kingdom of Italy. At this critical moment one of the regents, Antonio Onofrio, had a friendly meeting with Napoleon who subsequently supported Sammarinese liberty and the sovereign state, which was ideologically aligned with the French Revolution. Napoleon exempted its citizens from any type of taxation, gave them large quantities of wheat, but the cannons he promised never arrived. He also guaranteed to protect the independence of the republic and allowed them to expand their territory, which they declined. The state was officially recognized by Napoleon by the Treaty of Tolentino (1797) and with the fall of Napoleon by the Congress of Vienna (1815).

During the Italian unification movement San Marino aided its leader Giuseppe Garibaldi and his followers by providing them refuge. When Italy was unified, the two states signed conventions (March 22, 1862; reviewed in 1939 and 1971), which guarantee the independence, good relations, and trade of the Republic of San Marino.

Another positive development involved the Republic and President Abraham Lincoln. In 1861 shortly before the start of the Civil War, the Republic proposed an "alliance" between the two democratic nations and offered the president honorary Sammarinese citizenship. Lincoln accepted the offer in a letter of May 7th which concluded, "Although your dominion is small, your State is nevertheless one of the most honored, in all history. It has by its experience demonstrated the truth, so full of encouragement to the friends of Humanity, that Government founded on Republican principles is capable of being so administered as to be secure and enduring."

During the nineteenth century economic depression set into the Republic. There was a large increase in the birthrate, which widened the gap between agricultural and industrial development. The first emigration out of San Marino began. The first Sammarinesi sought seasonal employment in Tuscany, Rome, Genoa, and Trieste. Others sought jobs in France, Belgium, Germany, Austro-Hungarian Empire, and Greece. By the late 1890s they were looking across the Atlantic toward the Americas: United States, Argentina, and Uruguay. At this time whole families were uprooted and planned to permanently settle in the New World.

At the start of World War I, Italy tried to get San Marino to join her and declare war against Austria-Hungary. There was a fear that Austria with territory across the Adriatic Sea could use Sammarinese neutrality as a means of sending spies into Italy or using the newly constructed radiotelegraphic station. San Marino stood firm and maintained her neutrality. However two groups of volunteers did join Italian forces, one as combatants and the other operating a Red Cross field hospital. The latter action caused Austria-Hungary to break diplomatic relations with San Marino.

With the rise of Italian Fascism during the 1920s naturally the movement spread to San Marino. On August 10, 1922, Giuliani Gozi, a World War I veteran of the Royal Italian Army established the Fascist Party in San Marino. The fascists took control of the country (1923-1943) and used violence and intimidation against opponents as the Socialists. With a hardly noticed Jewish population, the party never adopted Anti-Jewish Laws as Italy did. The Fascist government undertook industrialization and public works projects with a railway connecting the country with Rimini and the development of the infrastructure, which paved the way for the tourist industry down to the present day.

The post-war era saw the Communists take advantage of the anger over the Allied bombing and the country was the first in Western Europe ruled by the Communist party through a democratic election in 1945. During these years it was obligatory to be a member of the party to get a job, which caused another out-migration of

Sammarinesi. San Marino was the first European nation to be won back from Communism in 1957.

Important developments took place in the late twentieth century. The Constitution of San Marino was promulgated in 1974. It consists of a number of legislative instruments, most significant being the Statute of 1600 and the Declaration of Citizen Rights of 1974 as amended in 2002.

San Marino was admitted into the Council of Europe on 16 November 1988 and joined the United Nations in 1992, which was long in coming. Since then the Republic has been a voice promoting human rights, peace, and solidarity.

In 1999 the Republic adopted the euro as its currency and also mints a special issue of the euro. In the early years of the twenty-first century San Marino became a tax haven for Italians and others. As a result over half dozen banks and other financial institutions developed. By 2017 the crisis of bad loans amounting to some $2 billion plagued the Republic and measures were taken to remedy the disaster.

Over the years the Republic of San Marino has maintained excellent relations with the United States. The Republic was recognized by the United States in May 1861. An extradition treaty was signed in 1906 and during World War I the United States unsuccessfully attempted to have Sammarinese prisoners of war released by Austria-Hungary. Consular relations were established in 1925. The Republic consistently supports American positions in the United Nations. In September 2006 President George W. Bush appointed Ronald P. Spogli Ambassador to Italy to serve concurrently as Ambassador to San Marino. Ambassador

Spogli was the first U.S. Ambassador to San Marino in the country's history. In July 2007, Ambassador Paolo Rondelli became San Marino's first ambassador to the United States.

Consular Offices

In 1929 New York banker F.M. Ferrari was honorary consul of the Republic of San Marino in New York City. Strangely in 1933 a native of Hungary, Alexander Konta, a New York banker, publicist, and former member of the State Parole Board held the position. By early 1947 Victor L. Anfuso, a New York borough attorney, served as consul into the 1950s. He played an important role traveling to the Republic to discuss war claims against the Allies' violation of San Marino's neutrality during the war. He also reported on the spread of Soviet Communism as part of their world order.

With the communist loss of San Marino in 1957, a year later in 1958 a prominent Manhattan attorney, Carroll A. Muccia, was the first fully accredited Sammarinese consul. The major event he faced was the visit by Frederico Bigi, the secretary of state of the Republic in 1959. Charles J. Re, a New Yorker of Italian descent, was next appointed consul general. He reported that there were some 3,000 Sammarinese citizens living in New York, New Jersey, Pennsylvania, and all of New England.

The other principal concentrations of Sammarinesi were Detroit and Sandusky. Italian-born sculptor Lelio De Ranieri was the first consul appointed in 1959. He saw his position as promoting the Republic of San Marino especially with school exhibits, developing—package tours to the

Republic. In 1965 Ranieri went back to the Old Country to serve as US consul to the Republic.[2]

Robert Balsimelli (1935-2020) served as consul general from 1982 until his passing. Of his service the Sammarinese Secretary of State for Foreign Affairs wrote he was one of those "tenacious and combative figures in affirming the uniqueness and privilege of citizenship that united San Marino citizens inside and outside the borders." He took pleasure in noting that his home-office in Elmont was "diplomatic territory". With his death the office continues. More on the Detroit office later.

Today there are four Sammarinese consular offices in the United States: Washington, D.C., New York, Michigan and Honolulu.[3]

Joseph Putti at San Marino Consulate.
Photo courtesy of author

Immigration to America

There were economic, social, and political reasons for the Sammarinesi to migrate from their charming and scenic homeland. The land had little to offer its folks. The ancient craft of quarrymen, which traced its origins to founder St. Marinus, had persisted, with little future to look forward to. Many of the citizens were sharecroppers or tenant farmers and had to bring the landowner the first crops and the best of everything. If you refused or brought inferior produce you could be put off the land and ostracized. Everyone was warned not to take in an ostracized family or the result would be similar (Uberti interview). Under these rules life was difficult. Tenants feared even the loss of a pear from a bushel basket. Young children rose very early in the morning and sold milk for the family. Young women sold eggs for a dowry. Furthermore, the tenant farmers were at the mercy of the environment and weather. They had neither control over the prices for goods they produced nor the unscrupulous nature of some landowners.

The social conditions were terrible as well. There were instances of thirteen people in a family living in a two-bedroom home without indoor plumbing. Women did their laundry in pools of water. In the frigid winters they had to break through ice to wash their clothes. They returned home with clean laundry but with cut and bleeding fingers and hands (Uberti).

Many families had large numbers of children. Due to economic demands, children between the ages of eight and twelve years were sold into "slavery" to farmers who needed child labor for minor tasks such as feeding cows at irregular hours and cleaning the fields.

Many survived in San Marino using their wits and learned skills. Ferucco Amati ran a taxicab service between the railroad station in Rimini and the mineral bathes in the hills. He would be intentionally late, telling his clients that he would rush them to the station and so they would not miss the train, which he did. The clients were so appreciative that they gave Ferucco large tips for making the train on time. Others operated shops, grocery stores, and restaurants. Alfredo Capicchioni owned a carpenter's shop and employed numerous workers who produced wooden doors and furniture. As a young teenager, Lucio Capicchioni worked for 2-3 years in his father's shop gaining important skills. He would be ready to enter the construction field, which needed trained skilled craftsmen and carpenters. Immigrants with mechanical skills and training were also readily employable when they arrived in America or other nations (Amati, Capicchioni).

Given the limited economic and social opportunity in San Marino men temporarily left for jobs in nearby locations, which would allow them to return to their families and friends. They first moved to Italian locations: Bologna, Liguria, Piedmont and Val D'Aosta, Ravenna, Rimini, Rome, and in the vicinity of Venice. Next Sammarinesi developed communities in Belgium, France (Grenoble and eastern France), and Switzerland. Then they moved off the European continent to: United States, Canada, Argentina, Brazil, Bahamas, Cuba, Mexico, Uruguay, and Egypt.[4]

On all accounts the Sammarinesi who immigrated were honest and humble people who brought with them a tradition of hard work. As Gabriele Bugli observed from experience, "skills and a lot of drive separate a lot of Sammarinese people from other ethnic groups. People with only a third-grade education were sharp, aggressive business-wise, very aggressive risk takers and they found that these attitudes worked well in America [and throughout the world]. They came with no language skills, without a knowledge of business and tax laws, but they survived and prospered" (Bugli). Giancarlo Ferri concluded that ninety-nine percent of the immigrants who migrated, left the Old Country with a fifth-grade education. There was little time for school since the children had to work the fields and care for the cattle and sheep as a result (Ferri).

Sammarinesi aboard the *Saturnia* in the 1950s. *Photo courtesy of author.*

11

Between 1923 and 1962 of the 12,030 Sammarinesi who were granted passports, 5,474 (45.5 percent) were: day laborers (1,866), laborers (1,747), and tenant farmers (1,861) while the remaining were craftsmen (995), housewives (3,007), skilled laborers (274) and "others" (2,280).[5] A study of the passports issued by the Republic shows the overall trends in immigration. During the decade of the 1920s (1923-1930) 2,873 Sammarinesi obtained passports, as many were uncomfortable with the rise of Mussolini's Fascists. Others heard of the rich economy in America especially the booming automobile industry in Detroit and its environs. Then due to the economic disaster of the Great Depression (1931-1939) immigration decreased to 1,539 and during World War II with the demand for industrial laborers throughout Nazi-dominated Europe some 2,706 left the Republic. In the decade after the war (1946-1957) when Communists controlled the country and demanded party membership for jobs, a "better life" and world economies were improving (1946-1956) 3,267 migrated, followed by another 1,642 through 1962.[6] Of the 12,030 passports issued over the years, largest number of immigrants was attracted to France followed by the United States.

With the removal of the Communists from the government, restrictions on employment possibilities came to an end after 1957. Thus there was less reason to leave the Republic. However, in the following years some Sammarinese immigrants immigrated to America.

It is interesting to note that by the 1960s travel shifted from steamships to jet planes. By the late twentieth century a developing economy in San Marino based on tourism, banking and finance provided opportunity, causing fewer to leave and has seen the continued re-migration to the Old Country especially as people retire.

Between 1956 and 1965 with the economic growth of most of Europe the Sammarinesi emigrated. Most of this emigration was directed towards Italy, followed by the United States, France, and Argentina. Switzerland, Belgium, Canada, and Brazil have accepted smaller groups. In the last quarter of the twentieth century emigration was halted and even reversed by the economic boom based on tourism, commerce, and financial structures in the Republic. However, by the turn of the twenty-first century there was another emigration, as young people sought jobs for their developed skills. Most of this emigration has been to Italy.

Migrating within the United States

When did the first Sammarinesi arrive in the United States? Unfortunately this is a difficult question to adequately answer because any number of Sammarinesi could have left their homeland and sailed to the Americas without being recorded. In most cases they were listed as coming from "Italy" and not from "the Republic of San Marino".

New York

The first known Sammarinesi to enter the United States began arriving in the second half of the nineteenth century, which began the era of grand European immigration. One the earliest ethnics was Giovanni Laico who arrived at the port of New York on February 9, 1874. He and his brother, Giuseppe were barbers and lived at 85 Broadway in New York City. In 1898 at the advanced age of 82, Giovanni became an American citizen. Onofrio Franmeni arrived in 1893 and was a bricklayer in Brooklyn in 1909, while Domenico Meloni arrived in late 1909 and found a job as a cook. Vincenzo Angeli and his wife Serafina Guidi Angeli arrived in 1908 at Ellis Island. They settled at 179 Prince Street in New York where they raised a family and Vince worked as a hat blocker.[7]

Not knowing about these earlier arrivals, a writer for the *Brooklyn Daily Eagle* of April 8, 1906 stated, "The only native of San Marino in this country is Mrs. Tina [Lombardi] Renganeschi of 139 West 10th Street," Manhattan.

The story of the Renganeschi family is intertwined and fascinating. Giovanni Renganeschi was born April 1866 in Pesora, Italy just southeast of San Marino. He married Tina Lombardi (1868-1935) in 1887 and the couple arrived separately to the United States in 1894 and 1895, and moved to the vicinity of Greenwich Village, which was attracting many immigrants. In 1898, Giovanni opened Renganeschi's Old Place Restaurant at 139 West 10th Street. When he opened his restaurant, foreign restaurants had been gaining in popularity and being close to Greenwich Village it became a favorite with artists and writers. Within the same building, Tina operated a boardinghouse called Albergo Titano (Hotel Titano) catering to Sammarinesi, Italians, and other newly arrived immigrants. In 1900 there were four Italian boarders staying at the boarding house: an artist, "artisan," college janitor, and a salesman. The boardinghouse became an important stop for arriving Sammarinesi and served as a safe and assimilative haven.

Tina also served as cashier in the restaurant and worked in the kitchen as well, sharing her culinary expertise and the dessert *zabaglione alla Tina* appeared on the menu in 1916. Obviously, Tina lived in a world of immigrants because in 1906, a decade after her arrival she did not speak English. The restaurant was considered one of the best-known restaurants in New York City at the time. The Renganeschis returned to Italy and San Marino on a trip and returned to New York in the fall of 1922. Five years later in his early 60s Giovanni decided to retire and sold his restaurant and moved to Brooklyn.[8]

The Renganeschi couple aided the second generation of Sammarinese family members to come to America.[9] In 1904, Tina's brother Giovanni Lombardi, a 40-year-old stone cutter had four children and one on the way with little hope for the family's future in San Marino. Tina and Giovanni Renganeschi paid for his and his son Bruno's passage to America. They arrived on January 19, 1905 and found immediate accommodations at Albergo Titano and proceeded to find jobs. Two years later Giovanni could pay the fare for the rest of the family to come to America. Eugenia traveled to Genoa with four children ages 4 through 14 and arrived in New York on March 20, 1907 and moved into the albergo. In 1910 Giovanni now known as John and family were living on King Street in Manhattan and he clerked in a liquor store. In these early years members of the family worked at Renganeschi's restaurant as an assistant cook and cashier.

John Sloan lived only two blocks from the restaurant and is known to have eaten there. On one occasion he was even joined by Robert Henri, a fellow artist of the Ashcan School of realistic painters. In 1912 Sloan painted, "Renganeschi's Saturday Night" (oil on canvas) where he explored the leisure activities of working-class women and the changing social mores of the twentieth century. Here he shows three women celebrating a night out exercising their newfound freedom to socialize in public without the need for male escorts. It is surprising to see a painting on the wall of Monte Titano. In 1916 Renganeschi used "Titano" as his cable address. Location: Art Institute of Chicago.

Bruno went from being a Sammarinese stonecutter to having a chauffeur's job driving the busy streets of New York City. He went on to become a master auto mechanic with his own shop. Over the years he and his wife lived in the Sammarinese neighborhood of Hempstead and Queens. He passed in 1981 at Passaic, New York. His second son, Julius (1893-1960) first found a position as an electrician and then also went into auto mechanics. In 1925 he partnered with Charles Renganeschi, a possible relative and operated a restaurant at 181 W. 10th Street in New York. By 1940 Julius owned his own restaurant continuing a family tradition. Daughter Santora married Hugo Del Fante in December 1919 and made their home on Staten Island. Hugo as a hatter, had a unique and dangerous occupation due to mercury poisoning. In 1920 eighteen-year-old Hamlet was a stenographer in a law office and a decade later he was the manager of a silk house and lived in Queens. The youngest in the family, Kino, who became known as George, in 1930 was a 24-year-old bachelor living with his parents and working as a restaurant cashier. It is interesting to note that no member of the family engaged in traditional Sammarinese occupations in construction, cement, or tile.[10]

In May 1926 Luigi Lombardi and his wife Zaira and son Gino along with Luigi's brother Mario arrived in New York. They boarded with the Lombardis' sister Tina and her husband, Giovanni at 139 W. 10th Street. They had continued welcoming Sammarinese immigrants.[11]

In the early days others found employment in New York City's many restaurants. Thus by the 1920s Sammarinesi joined the concentration of Italian immigrants who lived between 100th and 116th Streets in New York City. They sent their children to local public and Catholic schools where they could master the English language. Life in the noisy and crowded urban setting was difficult for a people used to relatively rural life in the Old Country. Climbing to the third story of an apartment building was a new experience, while gardens with flowers or vegetables were no longer a possibility. As a result they began to leave Manhattan Island and move into Brooklyn and the Bronx and many Sammarinesi were attracted to Queens.

Giovanni Giannini, A Success Story

The story of Sammarinese immigrant Giovanni Gianni (1924-2014) helps us understand how one Sammarinese dealt with coming to America. Giovanni grew up in San Marino and apprenticed as a carpenter-cabinet maker. When he was 24 years old his uncle in New York provided him with travel funds. Before he left, he married Maria Righi. In traditional fashion he stayed with his family in New York City before he got a room but had a job within two days of arriving. Soon he was making $36 a week after taxes. He was able to bring his wife over and the couple lived in Yorktown Heights, where they raised three children, and sent them to fine private schools. He and his wife were active in parish church and school affairs. Then he shared his agricultural wisdom with his grandchildren. As a cabinetmaker, Giovanni had an amazing talent for working with a lost art.[12]

Naturally a variety of jobs in the construction industry attracted many Sammarinese males because of their experiences at home. Brickwork was an important calling and others found immediate jobs as ditch diggers and construction workers on the expanding subway system. As new public and private buildings were being constructed workers from general laborers, to tile layers and terrazzo workers were needed.

In a surprising move 24-year-old Anthony Bruschi who had emigrated five years before was an insurance agent in 1930. In Manhattan Fortunato Bruschi and his brother, Natalino arriving in the late 1920s were employed as laborers in an electrical equipment factory. In Queens a fellow was a watchmaker in an electric factory.

If New York City proved to be oppressive, many of the Sammarinesi heard of more rural and bucolic Long Island. In the 1880s Long Island had attracted a large Italian community scattered through a variety of communities in the vicinity of Oyster Bay, Elmont, and Westbury. These immigrants found work in the stone and sand quarries, in construction, small factories, on the Long Island Railroad, in nurseries and on large estates in the area.[13] Once the Italian communities were created, it was natural that Sammarinesi would have a new home or an ethnic "nest" as well. In the 1920s the first Sammarinesi settled in Elmont on Long Island. To the east, Westbury went through a frenzied pace of building and needed laborers during the 1920s and Sammarinesi filled the demand. Still others found jobs working for wealthy people on Long Island as chauffeurs, servants, domestics, and gardeners.[14]

When Giancarlo Ferri arrived in Long Island, he boarded with his older brother and had immediate help with jobs. Domenico Filippi also boarded with him and without a knowledge of English took every job that was available. One of them worked for J & B Tool & Die and understood engineering blueprints and worked there many months. On weekends they would work on other construction jobs so that no day was wasted. His first paycheck was $33 per week, which was considered big money at that time (Ferri).

New arrivals were attracted by ready employment and settled north of New York City proper. Larchmont, New Rochelle, Mamaroneck, Tuckahoe and even Putnam County farther to the north became home to Sammarinesi. On July 12, 1929 twelve Sammarinesi arrived at Ellis Island. Four went to Detroit to be with relatives. However others like Secondo Minicucci first joined his cousin Ottaviano, who had sponsored him in Mamaroneck and by the spring of 1930 had moved ten miles to the west to Tuckahoe, Westchester County, New York. He boarded in the home of an Italian along with two other Sammarinesi – Marino Belloni and Luigi Becchari – they were all laborers on construction jobs.[15]

Although farming did not attract many Sammarinesi a few went in that direction. In New Jersey, Marlboro Township was home to truck farmers and during mid- twentieth century it was the largest national producer of potatoes and had large tomato and poultry operations. Giovanni Benedettino and Ernesto Cello who arrived in 1926 found work as farm laborers working for an Italian truck farmer, Vincent Losito. Thus they were able to leave the confines of New York City and ply a trade they knew in the Old Country.[16]

A scattering of Sammarinesi found their way into western New York state once again following Italian migration and chain migration. They settled in Niagara Falls with its large Italian immigrant population and where industrial jobs were readily available. Joseph Frisoni (1893-1976) arrived in the United States in 1912 as a nineteen-year-

Adamo Gatti in New Haven, Connecticut circa 1950 doing his own laundry. He lived in Connecticut with a cousin's family (the De Marini family) for 3 years, before moving to Detroit, Michigan where he was joined by his wife and 4 daughters in 1954. *Photo courtesy Lisette Selva.*

old and got a job at Oldbury Electro Chemical Company. By the spring of 1930 Joseph and Anthony had arrived with their families and found work at the chemical plant. Dino, Anthony's son, trained as a tailor and opened his own business locally. This tiny colony of Sammarinesi was known to Detroiters because at a later date Lucio Capicchioni's uncle Marino moved from Detroit to Buffalo as an automobile salesman. Anacleto, a tile man, followed his brother to Buffalo as well.[17] Others went northward and settled in New England.

Sandusky-Kelleys Island Experience

Sandusky and Erie County in northern Ohio hold a special place in the annals of the Sammarinese diaspora, as this is where they first settled in the interior of America. The first Sammarinesi were attracted to Sandusky and Erie County due to the Italian population, many of whom were from Emilia-Romagna province, neighboring San Marino. The Italians had been arriving since the late nineteenth century and in 1900 numbered 110. During the next decades joined by Sammarinesi the number grew to 507 making them the second largest ethnic group in Erie County after the 2,388 Germans. For Sammarinesi, who were primarily stonecutters, New York offered them few jobs quarrying, while Erie County was home to stone and limestone quarries that needed hundreds of unskilled laborers.

According to oral tradition, beginning in 1907, three Sammarinesi from Montegiardino left the Republic seeking work in America. They were three members of the Casali family including the leader of the group called, "Tribréll". These three Casali started Sammarinese immigration to Ohio quarries that continued until the outbreak of World War I, facilitated by direct-service from New York over the New York Central Railroad.[18]

The Kelleys Island Lime and Transport Company operated between 1896 and the early 1960s. During its heyday it was .the largest producer of limestone and lime products in the area. Fishing and vineyards producing wine and grape juice rivaled the quarry work. The quarry providing soft limestone for the developing steel industry where limestone was used as flux in the steel making process. The ethnic composition on the island was Hungarian, Irish, Slovenian, Slovak, Polish, Italian, and Sammarinese.

The story of Pasquale Zanotti is illustrative of migratory patterns set by many Sammarinesi seeking economic opportunity. Zanotti first moved to France where he worked for a year and then in 1920 followed his brother, Lorenzo who had arrived in Sandusky a year earlier. Pasquale worked in Wagner Quarry and then had an opportunity to go to Port Clinton and work in a gypsum quarry where he could do piece work and make more money. He stayed there for seven years and in 1927 returned to San Marino where he got married. Then he returned to the United States with the intention of sending for his wife and son, Secondo. With the coming of the Depression, having saved a little money he returned to San Marino in 1930, bought a farm and cultivated wheat and olives. Happy with the farm he never returned to the United States. His brother, Lorenzo returned to San Marino in 1936. It was not until 1949 that

Secondo came to the United States. His future wife Pierine Suzzi arrived separately and soon married Secondo, as they were next-door neighbors in the Old Country.

Vincenzo Moscioni was another Sammarinese who was attracted to Kelleys Island. First he sought work in France during the 1920s and then decided to immigrate to the United States having heard of better possibilities. He settled on Kelleys Island and worked as a fireman under a licensed stationary engineer. In the 1920s Poles and Slovaks maintained the equipment. The Poles operated the cranes and did the blasting in the quarry. The Sammarinesi did a variety of jobs. The Boccis worked on the loading dock where they emptied cars into a pit where the conveyor belt loaded the stone onto ships. Many of them were brakemen on the railroad, while others operated the electric shovels or labored around the cranes as oilers. The work was hard and men had to work on cold winter days and through the hot, humid summers. Accidents were common and blindness was possible due to the flying stone. Most of the Sammarinesi worked in the quarry, but there was one fellow Marino Miani who was a shoe repairman (Moscioni).

A look at life on Kelleys Island provides us with an intimate picture of a relative isolated Sammarinese community as opposed to those in Detroit and New York. The workers had their own homes, which were rented from the quarry company. The Sammarinesi lived close to each other and interacted. They kept large vegetable gardens and some of them like the Moscionis raised large fields of potatoes. Many kept a cow for milk and butter and a hog. The mothers and children took care of the farm duties, tending the gardens

Kelleys Island Quarry. *Photo courtesy of Sandusky Public Library.*

and milking the cows, while the fathers would work in the gardens after coming home from work. In the fall the Sammarinesi would get together and help each other slaughter their hogs. Vincenzo Moscioni was the chief animal slaughterer during the 1930s. The meat was cut up and preserved in lard-lined crocks while sausage and salami were made. For a while the Moscionis kept a small steer. Most of the Sammarinese families made their own wine and some of them distilled the grape skins into *grappa*, a potent but popular liquor. In all cases the families maintained their small gardens and animals through team effort, as did the general community.

Life on the island was peaceful and quiet and all of the ethnic groups got along with each other. St. Michael Catholic Church was available to the Sammarinesi although in the

25

1920s the pastor Fr. Joseph Maerder was German-born to serve the large German Catholic community. The immigrant families would get together monthly at one of five different homes. Joseph Miani was an accordion player and kept the evening lively. At other times they played bocce and various Italian card games were extremely popular. It was not common for the Sammarinese families to travel to Sandusky as the island had everything, which they needed.

The kids grew up on an island paradise. They were always going "under the fence" and playing in an isolated part of the quarry before they were chased away. They swam either in Lake Erie or in "the Cut" a pool in the quarry. Fishing was popular and many of the Sammarinese kids could only wish for bicycles or ice skates, due financial restraints.

The Kelleys Island quarry began to decline in the late 1930s as they ran out of soft limestone and there was competition from quarries at Marblehead on the mainland. By 1941 most of the Sammarinesi had left the island for the mainland. Some found employment in quarries like the Wagner Quarry in Perkins Township and others found better paying jobs in the local foundries.

With the start of World War II, jobs in industry were in demand and plentiful. Many of the Kelleys Island Sammarinesi found jobs in the Farrell-Cheek Steel Company[19] and others worked at Delphi-E&C, a ball and roller bearing manufacturer. In Sandusky, the Lyman Boat Works was an important industry long known for their wooden boats. A key person at Lyman was Marino Giovagnoli who was a 1920s immigrant and became a foreman. When the Sammarinesi arrived after World War II he hired many of them at the boat works. This would set the stage for future immigration after the war.

Detroit Communities

The Sammarinese immigrants never arrived in large enough numbers to create their own "Little San Marino" in Detroit or elsewhere. However, they were at home with the large Italian communities that developed in Metro Detroit.

The first large contingent of Sammarinesi was located within Little Italy, which centered in the vicinity of Gratiot and McDougall Streets in downtown Detroit. There were a variety of Italian restaurants, coffee houses, saloons, shops and especially Bonaldi's bookstore, which was popular as an outlet for Italian language newspapers and magazines, where Sammarinesi congregated in the evenings.[20] Their spiritual needs were cared for at two local Italian Catholic ethnic parishes: Holy Cross and San Francesco.

Among the early Sammarinese arrivals to Little Italy, a characteristic so associated with them manifested itself– exclusiveness. Although they were surrounded by an overwhelming number of Italians, especially Venetians, their brother tile workers, they maintained their strong, independent Sammarinese identity, as we shall see.[21]

In the 1920s, Metro Detroit and neighboring communities attracted people from throughout the United States and immigrants because of the automobile industry. With this development, many of the Sammarinesi migrated to Detroit from either the Old Country or from Sandusky and New York. Jobs were readily available in the auto industry, especially at Ford Motor's massive Rouge River plant near

Dearborn and Oakwood. Some of the Sammarinesi were trained as mechanics in the Old Country and found that more technical jobs were available to them. For the unskilled there were positions on the assembly line. The demand for housing for the thousands of people who descended upon Detroit seeking jobs in the auto plants strained the construction industry that needed unskilled and skilled laborers.

In the Detroit area construction was the dominant occupation of Sammarinese immigrants of which seventy-five percent were contractors or in the building trades. Only 20 percent were connected with restaurants or service industries and five percent were employed in tool and die, etc. (Ferri). Some Sammarinesi, who came to Detroit as mechanics left auto jobs and moved into more profitable construction work even if it meant working out-of-doors.

As it has been seen earlier most Sammarinese came as former laborers and tenant farmers. Occupations of Sammarinesi were varied and diverse depending on their location. In New York City the first Sammarinesi became involved in the service industry and opened restaurants. However, the city and suburbs were booming in the early twentieth century and construction positions and general labor were readily available. The field was wide-open.

The construction trades are complex. Basic carpenters found low-level jobs and then got into dry walling and became skilled craftsmen. There were cabinetmakers and finish carpenters, who installed crown-molding, baseboards, windows, stairs and other features of a structure that require aesthetic appeal. Electrical work and plumbing attracted others (Babboni).

Terrazzo, tile, and cement work attracted Sammarinesi. Many were hired by Venetian craftsmen to work as tile men and terrazzo workers. This was labor intensive and was costly as the terrazzo was placed and then grinding had to be done. You could not do high-volume work with this procedure (Bugli). Flat work consists of setting cement for foundations, garages, basements, and driveways on a residential scale. No vertical work was done. Others were bricklayers and Formica men. As a result, newly arrived Sammarinesi readily found basic jobs, worked their way up the economic ladder, and developed their own businesses and became competitors of their former employers. As Lucio Capicchioni concluded, "It's a way of life" (Bugli, Capicchioni).

Success stories in construction are frequent. Marino Casadei (1907-1992) was one of these. He worked in tile and then in 1953 he established Dearborn Tile Construction or the "Tile Company."

In the 1940s and 1950s the Titanus Cement Wall Company the biggest Sammarinese-owned company in Detroit, started with three partners from San Marino: Enzo "Cino" Mularoni, Gigi Vincenti, and Pete Dell'Olmo. During these years of immigration these companies provided jobs for the new arrivals and allowed them to get a start in American society (Ferri, Dall'Olmo).

The career of John Malpeli (1901-1991) is an insightful example of how one Sammarinese immigrant made his way up the American economic ladder through home construction. Malpeli was born in San Marino and trained as a mechanic until he was eighteen and traveled to Genoa to board the steamer *Re d'Italia* arriving in New York City on February 3,

1920. He traveled to Detroit, where he got a job in construction and five years later married Anna Melo an Italian-American woman from Illinois. He was a cement contractor in 1930. The Malpelis were renting a home for $60 a month on Cheyenne Street and took in a boarder, Joseph Vincent who worked as a building cement mixer.

His financial situation flourished and a decade later Malpeli owned a $12,000 home in Dearborn and had opened the Malpeli Construction Company. He was partnered with Albert Mularoni and developed land in Dearborn.

With the economic boom in Detroit caused by the outbreak of World War II, Malpeli began to develop suburban housing. In May 1941 he had 150 homes available on Grandville Avenue between Southfield and Rouge Park selling for $3,950. Construction continued through the war and since wood was a rationed item he built with brick and advertised sixty-two new homes available for sale or rent described as "six room brick, tile features, colored bathroom features and full basement." By February 1943 of the 250 homes they constructed only six were unsold and available. A decade later he was developing San Marino Villa at Inkster and 12 Mile offering 123 homes at $30,000-$50,000. He also developed San Marino Meadows, a large subdivision on M-59 just west of M-23. In Florida he developed San Marino Pines for snowbirds spending the winter in mobile homes on Lake San Marino.[22]

A contemporary in the construction trade was Bruno L. Pasquali (1929-1998) of Commerce Township, Michigan who was born in San Marino and immigrated to the United States in 1949. By the following year he had established Pasquali

Construction Company and became president and CEO of the company and was joined by his sons. As a licensed builder the company constructed hundreds of homes in the Tri-County Area.[23]

One of the outstanding Sammarinese homebuilders in Metro Detroit was Dino Crescentini (1947-2008), who was an excellent example of a conscientious and hard-working immigrant. Born in San Marino, where he learned finish carpentry, he immigrated to the United States with his family in 1969. He established CBC Builders in Rochester Hills with a passion for excellence and quality construction always wanting to give his customers even in tract homes "a little something extra to the job." Special building challenges of this finish carpenter were his passion. His quality work attracted "niche people" – business and sports figures - who demanded the best in their custom homes. In 2000 he was building homes in Orchard Ridge in Oakland Township where lots sold for $1.8 million and homes sold as high as $3.4 million.[24]

Life for the immigrants was one of adjusting to and eventually assimilating into American society as evidenced by Frank Paoletti who came to the United States in 1949 and settled in Detroit. He arrived with about ten to fifteen Sammarinesi who were of similar age and given the small size of the Republic most of the immigrants knew each other. They would board together or within the vicinity and they knew each other even if they did not know the exact street address. Lacking a telephone or automobile an individual walked up the street and usually encountered the person he was seeking.

Restaurants

Although most Sammarinesi focused on aspects of the construction industry especially in Michigan, there was a tradition among a small number of them to engage in the restaurant business. Some of them left construction and tried their hands in the restaurant business, but quickly found that the hours were long and the work less rewarding. Many of these people returned to outdoor construction work, one fellow said "the job ended at 4:30" whereas restaurant work would end in the wee hours. As opposed to related groups like the Italians, most of the Sammarinesi generally stayed away from the service industries, but some got involved.

As we have seen the first Sammarinese restaurateurs were Tina Lombardi Renganeschi and her husband Giovanni who opened a successful restaurant in Greenwich Village in the early twentieth century. After 1947 some of the arriving Sammarinesi got into the food service business starting as waiters, cooks, and even dishwashers.

Guilio's Café between McDougall and Gratiot in Detroit was one of these early restaurants. Antonia Cardinali was a waitress at Guilio's and she bought the business in 1947 renaming it Cardinali's Restaurant. Her husband worked in a factory and she ran a successful operation. When she could not get a liquor license because the café was too close to a church, she served wine in paper cups and even visiting policemen stopped by and asked for "cold coffee." Antonia was in business for forty years (Putti).

Giovanni and Iris Bugli immigrated to Detroit and Giovanni did cement work in the day and to make ends meet washed dishes at night. His wife was restless since they did not have children yet, and they opened Johnny's Pizzarena on Jefferson Blvd. in Detroit's East Side, one of the first in the area. Both of them enjoyed Italian cooking and the pizzeria was successful. Giovanni worked in the restaurant in the evenings and expanded it into a full-service restaurant. However, the call of outdoor work returned and Giovanni sold the restaurant and developed Metropolitan Cement, which was eventually taken over by his son Marco (Bugli).

The Berardi family was associated with the Cedar Park amusement park in Sandusky and the restaurant business. In 1939 Al Berardi worked in the penny arcade selling skee-ball tickets working sixty plus hours a week making $11 a week.

Three years later Berardi along with a partner built the first French fry stand at the park. After a few years, Al's partner left to pursue other interests. So along with Al's mother, Erosia (known by all as Momma Berardi) the Berardis continued to sell their hand-washed, hand-cut French fries. Over the years the French fries won four Readers' Choice Awards. They also owned and operated many of Cedar Point's first rides such as the flying scooter, the pretzel dark ride (now known as the Monster), the tilt-a-whirl and others. Secondo also helped and opened the Spaghetti Hut at the park in 1947 selling spaghetti dinners for 75 cents. By the 1970s and two French Fry stands later, the Berardis were selling as many as two tons of potatoes in a single day. Another family member had a successful waffle stand at Cedar Point. In 1978, after almost 40 years of success the Berardi family and the original Berardi French Fries left

Cedar Point when the Cedar Fair Entertainment Company eliminated private enterprises in the park (Crooks).

After they left Cedar Point the Berardi family continued in the restaurant business. Berardi's Wagon Wheel specialized in fresh roast beef sandwiches, French fries, and Roseanne Berardi's famous home-made pies. It was eventually sold. There was the BZB restaurant located nearby, which opened in 1962. Today Berardi's Family Kitchen in Sandusky continues as a culinary feature of the community known for its fries and pies. In neighboring Huron, Berardi's Family Restaurant, which opened in 1979 also continues the family tradition.

Out of Little Italy & into Suburbia

As with the Italian community, the Sammarinesi used Gratiot Street as a highway out of Little Italy. In the 1920s some Sammarinesi moved to "Cacalupo" an Italian community at Eight Mile near the streetcar barns and yards. As they assimilated and became affluent, the Sammarinesi continued a northward migration into suburbia. The vast majority remained on the East Side (east of Woodward Avenue) of Detroit. They first moved into East Detroit (now Eastpointe) and St. Clair Shores following Italian-Americans. Today some 75 percent of the Sammarinesi live in Sterling Heights and neighboring Troy, Warren, Rochester, and Rochester Hills. At present, descendants of the immigrants are found throughout Metro Detroit (Putti, Uberti, Bugli).

The second concentration of Sammarinesi was located in another Italian neighborhood, the Oakwood-Fort Street neighborhood in the southwestern corner of Detroit. It was developed in the 1920s by Italians and South Slavs and turned into a quiet, tree-lined neighborhood on the banks of the Rouge River. Unfortunately, this green oasis was encircled by an underground salt mine, gas and oil refineries, chemical plants, the looming Ford Rouge plant to the north and surrounded by rail lines. The Italian and Sammarinese Catholics were served by Our Lady of Mt. Carmel Catholic church, which was established in 1928 and is now closed.

September 1954, somewhere on the Atlantic Ocean, aboard the *Andrea Doria*, (which sank two years later) headed to New York Harbor, where a family friend put the family on a train to Detroit, where father was awaiting the group. (L to R) Travelling companions- name forgotten, Roseann Gatti (14 years), Lisette Gatti (12 years), Tina Gatti- mother (39 years), Maria Gatti (6 years), Marisa Gatti (8 years). *Photo courtesy of Lisette Selva.*

The first Sammarinesi were attracted to this area around 1949 with the third major migration of Sammarinesi fostered by chain migration. The immigrants were sponsored by friends or relatives and found this area with its Italian population and many potential jobs conducive to settlement. Some of the Sammarinesi who migrated north from Sandusky along the then Dixie Highway (now I-75) found this enclave a welcoming community and stayed.

In the late 1950s there were forty to fifty Sammarinese families living here and many of them took in recently arrived single Sammarinese boarders. These boardinghouse accommodations were a safe and warm haven for these recent arrivals struggling to learn the English language and assimilate into American life. In this oasis they could enjoy traditional food and good cheer with countrymen.

These Sammarinesi worked in various industries including the Ford Motor Company and as contractors and tile workers. One family got into the restaurant business. In the 1950s they were paid $21 a week and worked five days a week, ten-to-twelve-hour days, finding part-time work on weekends. They had little time to worry about the amenities of life. Being hard workers, many Sammarinesi made their "fortunes" under these horrendous work schedules and left Fort-Oakwood and returned to the Old Country. There they invested in seaside restaurants in Rimini, others bought shops and still others purchased farmland and returned to the soil.

The Sammarinesi who remained in the quiet tree-lined enclave of Oakwood-Fort developed families and remained in the district until the heavy, unceasing, unpleasant industrial

"c. 1956. All the men pictured in photo save for one are Sammarinese men that had left their families in San Marino. Some were boarders, others came to eat Sunday dinner with us." *Photo courtesy of Lisette Selva.*

pollution– smelly acrid fumes from the surrounding industries drove them to the suburbs beginning in the late 1960s. Many of the Sammarinesi who lived in this community called it "Okud" having changed "Oakwood" into their dialect. This caused problems for individuals not familiar with their dialect.

Some forty years later Sammarinese-Americans live in neighboring West Side communities like Melvindale and southward into Allen Park, Trenton, Flat Rock and neighboring communities.[25]

While most of the Sammarinesi moved around Metro Detroit over the years, others had either first settled or moved to Canada. A small community has developed in Windsor, Ontario across the Detroit River from Detroit. During the winter, retirees or "snowbirds" leave Michigan for several months to enjoy the leisure and golf afforded them in sunny warm Florida (Paoletti).

Trans-Mississippi West

Although Sammarinesi concentrated themselves in Metro Detroit, Sandusky and New York City and its environs, it is incorrect to think that they limited their settlement patterns. Seeking economic stability, others spread across the United States usually associating with the larger Italian immigrant populations. As we move away from the traditional settlement sites of Sammarinese immigrants, in the trans-Mississippi West we find them in a number of railroad center communities.

Out West, Montana became a destination for a number of Sammarinesi. Members of the Bugli family joined the Italian community in Missoula working on the Northern Pacific Railroad. Zachary Bugli (1868-1926) was the pioneer. He immigrated in 1907 and then returned to San Marino in 1909 and 1913 to accompany his sons Joseph and Marino back to Missoula. In 1914 his wife, Teresa brought Mary, Catherine and Peter to Missoula. In 1920 even at 62 years of age Zachary was working as a track laborer for the Northern Pacific Railroad, until he lost his life in an accident several years later.[26]

His son Joseph A. Bugli (1891-1985) arrived from San Marino at 16 years of age in 1909 and attended business college. He owned and operated the Broadway Market and was a member of the Musicians Union, Local 498 for fifty years. He played in the Missoula City Band and the Elks Band. Marino "Mike" (1896-1985) served in World War I, in late 1918 got married, and trained at barber school in Great Falls. He operated a barber shop in Missoula and in retirement moved to the Bitter Root valley where he did occasional barbering. The third son Peter (1906-1964) became a farmer in the Bitter Root Valley where he operated a sawmill when he cleared his land. He played a major role in the life of the community. Loving the out-of-doors he served with the U.S. Forest Service until his passing. Their sister Catherine married James Canton and also lived in the valley on a farm. The other sister Mary was married in 1922 to August Antonini, an immigrant of San Leo, Italy near the Republic. He was a coal miner in Pekin, Illinois until retiring to Los Angeles.[27] The offspring of Zachary had numerous children and their descendants continue to live in Missoula and vicinity where they continue to play important roles on the life of their communities. By not leaving the area they have created a family colony of Sammarinesi and Sammarinese-Americans, whose stories are to be found in the area newspapers. Today, members of the family are to be found throughout the Northwest.[28]

Other Sammarinesi found their way to Siskiyou County in northern California where they worked jobs in sawmills and on the Southern Pacific Railroad. Gaspare Zanotto, an Italian, who worked in a lumber yard and dry kiln in 1930 and 1940 was married to Elisa Gardenghi, a housewife, who was Sammarinese.[29]

The census also shows an interesting situation. At Edgewood 3 miles north of Weed, there was 21-year-old Sammarinese, also named Marco Gardenghi working as a section laborer boarding with others and the section boss, Joe Secatto.[30]

Dunsmuir in the shadow of Mount Shasta, located some twenty miles south attracted some Sammarinesi. Here the Southern Pacific Railroad had a major transit point, where extra steam locomotives were added to assist trains up the grade to the north. Sammarinesi Azzolini Bombini (1879-1946) and his wife, Guiseppina Gardenghi, arrived in New York in 1924 and they were scheduled to go to the now "lost" town of Kilt, California to join relative, Gaspare Zanotto. In 1930, the Bombini family was joined by relatives 42-year-old Frederico Gardenghi and sixteen-year-old Marco who had arrived in 1929. Both obtained jobs as laborers in the Southern Pacific shops along with Sammarinesi who were working as machinist and truck builder. By 1940, the latter two had migrated from the northern wilderness.

The Great Depression

The period between 1929 and 1939 was difficult for Sammarinese immigrants along with the rest of the nation. The Depression put an end to the boom times in Detroit and construction came to a standstill.

Before the full impact of the Depression was felt some last groups of Sammarinesi arrived. On December 20, 1929 two months after the stock market crash, a group of Sammarinesi including families arrived and settled in New

York City. In January 1930, a group of ten Sammarinesi arrived in New York. They found their way to Detroit and Sandusky while others stayed in New York City, New Rochelle, and Westbury. All of this was again conducted by way of family chain migration. Most arrived as laborers although one was a mechanic and another a chauffeur. They would survive through the economic struggle.

Census records for 1940 provide us with glimpses into the weeks immigrants worked and wages earned. Virgilio Michalotti, a building cabinetmaker in New Rochelle, New York worked for 39 weeks in 1939 and made $1600. In bustling New York City Albert and Maria Debiagi owned a liquor store that was open for 48 weeks. In an interesting shift John Burgagni worked for 52 weeks for $800 as a watch factory packer while his wife Antonia, a dressmaker, worked for 50 weeks and made $1200. At Sandusky John Muratori, a grinder at an iron foundry, worked for only 25 weeks. In Detroit Sante Putti was a scrap baler for an automotive company and worked a full year for $1500 but maintained his finances by taking in three boarders: creamery bottle washer working 50 weeks for $1450; a fellow working in automotive heat treatment for 28 weeks for $550 and a machine operator working a mere 16 weeks for $450. Proprietors like building contractor John Malpeli and tile and terrazzo maker Humberto Mularoni worked the full year but did not include their salaries, which were probably significant. This is a mere glimpse but shows the impact of the Depression on individuals. Weeks of unemployment varied with the jobs and how they were affected by the economy.[31] Those who lost their jobs turned to Federal assistance and worked for the Works

Progress Administration, where their construction experience was readily used.

Possessing their strong tradition of close ethnic ties, the Sammarinesi were strong and people could turn to family and friends for support. There might not be food on the table and then miraculously food appeared. Primo Bizzocchi owned a home near Eastern Market in Detroit and took in two boarders, whom his wife fed and washed their clothes. This continued as a source of assistance and some financial gain. Arthur Amati's parents moved in with David Zaffarani's family who needed help. The Amati income was spread out and the Zaffaranis were assisted (Amati). Returning to their farming tradition in the Old Country many weathered the Depression with family gardens. Others turned to the profitable manufacture and sale of illegal liquor during Prohibition and widows got into marketing it (Babboni, Bizzochi).

Before the Depression the boardinghouse had become the domain of women. The first roomers paid $5 per week and later $10-$15 for room and board. During the Depression this could mean some women could make at least $520 annually, but then unemployment meant boarders might not be able to pay the minimum (Umberti).

When all else failed, some Sammarinesi decided to return to San Marino, a land that they knew. At least if they were struggling economically, they were surrounded by family and friends (Crooks, Zanotti).

World War II

World War II affected the people of San Marino and Sammarinese-Americans. The war terminated immigration from San Marino to the Americas. Nazi Germany sought laborers and Sammarinesi were available. In 1943 during the middle of the war, 456 (89%) Sammarinese went to Italy; 28 (5%) to France; 29 (6%) to other places; and two to Switzerland.

Deteriorating Italian-US diplomatic conditions had a direct impact on the Balsimelli family. Arturo Balsimelli was a secretary-clerk at the Italian consulate office in New York City. On June 21, 1941, all American consulates in Germany and Italy were ordered closed. President Franklin Roosevelt retaliated by closing their consular offices in the United States and ordered all consular officials and propaganda agents to leave the country on July 15. The Balsimelli Family consisting of Arturo's wife Iris and two children, Rose Marie and Robert joined five hundred officials who boarded the *West Point*, which provided safe passage to neutral Lisbon, Portugal. From Lisbon the Balsimellis journeyed to San Marino where they spent the war years.[32]

In the United States many Sammarinese men and women joined the military and were sent overseas. Most of the Sammarinesi served in the U.S. Army and a few were in the Navy and served in Alaska. They served their country and some lost their lives in the defense of freedom (Uberti).

There were Italian prisoners of war in Detroit located at Fort Wayne. Italians and Sammarinesi had parties for them and Sunday dinners. They were usually accompanied by an Army guard who joined in the dinners. Two Sammarinese girls married Italian P.O.W.s, but unfortunately lost their Sammarinese citizenship as a result (Uberti).

The Berardi Brothers

The story of the Berardi brothers exemplifies the love of America and Sammarinese liberty. Robert (1922-1945) and Nello (1925-1944) were born in San Marino and immigrated with their parents, Adam and Teresa in July 1927 to Sandusky, Ohio. They grew up, becoming bi-lingual and engaged in high school life. Robert attended Bowling Green State University for three years majoring in business administration. When called for duty he enlisted as his brother had done earlier in the U.S. Army. The brothers planned on meeting on leave and return to San Marino their birthplace. Then dual tragedy struck. Nello, a private in the 7th Infantry, 3rd Division, was wounded in the Battle of Anzio south of Rome and succumbed on May 29, 1944. He is buried at Nettuno, Italy. His brother, Robert, a sergeant with the 407th Infantry, 102 Division was killed on February 24, 1945 as the 407th Division entered Germany from the Netherlands. He is buried at Margraten, Netherlands. Both men had received Purple Hearts and were the first double causalities from Sandusky. In 1961 the Republic of San Marino established a monument in Castello Fiorentino Cemetery recalling the sacrifice of "two young heroes."

During the war with construction at a near standstill Sammarinesi found industrial jobs in the "Arsenal of Democracy." Automobile companies switched over to tank, bomber, munitions, and related manufacture and workers were in demand. Giacomo Putti worked for the Ford Motor

Company and in a steel mill, while his brothers Carlo and Sante also worked for Ford. However, contractor John Malpeli, possibly using cement and brick as wood was considered a war materiel, developed subdivisions for the army of war workers that descended on Detroit and vicinity. Down in Sandusky, Theresa Berardi did war-related work at the Barr Rubber Company.

World War II saw the Republic of San Marino declare its neutrality and over 100,000 refugees sought asylum in the Republic. Those who remained in San Marino thought they would be free of involvement in the war because of its neutral stand. However, the Putti family saw money sent by their father abruptly end once Italy and the United States were at war. External support was gone and due to the war, which greatly disrupted life, there were few means of support and everyone survived by "living hand-to-mouth." However, for most of the war fighting was at a distance, but this changed in the latter part of 1944.

As the Allies pushed up the Italian Peninsula they encountered German defenses at the Gothic Line, which ran across Italy just south of San Marino. On June 26, 1944 believing the Germans had occupied San Marino the Royal Air Force "accidentally" bombed the country killing thirty-five people. A few weeks later a small German force violated neutrality and entered the country to monitor communications and as artillery observers from the hills.

The war had come to San Marino. Homes were seized by the German army as housing for officers and soldiers. People survived by living with family and friends or finding sleeping quarters in crowded nearby railroad tunnels. The

Ferri family hid their valuables in a small room and then masoned it over. To make it look old they covered the walls with charcoal and tar. Stores were empty as they had been throughout the war and the Germans found little to take (Putti, Ferri).

On September 17, the British 4th Indian Infantry Division entered the country and routed the Germans and on September 20 the fighting was over, conditions stabilized and Sammarinese defense forces took over. Post-war immigrants brought these stories with them to Michigan, San Marino had survived.

All of Europe was devastated by the war and the Republic of San Marino was no different. In November 1945 members of the San Marino Club shipped an impressive 5.25 tons in twenty-two cases to San Marino consisting clothes, shoes, cloth, needles and thread. Two years later Detroit Sammarinesi continued to send packages of warm clothing for the winter and other needed goods. In Detroit women cleared basement ping-pong tables to organize the goods to be sent to San Marino (Uberti).

The Tale of Two Consuls

Two Sammarinese consuls have interesting stories. Joseph Putti's father James had immigrated to the United States in 1926 and settled in Detroit but due to family concerns Joseph (1925-2015) did not emigrate and then World War II interfered. When Mr. Putti arrived in 1947, his sister found him a landscaping job, which was in line with his agricultural training as a youth. He was paid $1.00 per hour and worked at it for three months. Then he found a construction job working for a tile contractor and was so employed until 1954. In a typical development, Putti went into cement work and worked on his own until 1973 and eventually purchased American Concrete Wall where he employed 50 workers. In 1987 he was appointed the Sammarinese consul in Detroit.

Brooklyn-born Roberto Balsimelli (1935-2020) was six years old when his family had to return to San Marino in 1941. After the war his father sent him back to New York to seek a new life and employment. He returned to New York where his first job was delivering cases of wine to local shops. Then he went to work in a machine shop and eventually opened his own shops in Farmingdale and Deer Park on Long Island. He was appointed consul for the Republic of San Marino and held the position until his passing.

Ethnic Survival & Community

Sammarinesi arrived with few material goods, but they realized that they had each other and united they could work together. As Walter Babboni fondly recalled, "they never knew anything else but it was like [being] in a cocoon."

In a number of different venues we can observe the tight bonding among Sammarinese people. Although in different worlds, they maintained family values especially when raising their children who were taught the history and value of their Old Country heritage. This was especially true in Clinton Township, home to many Sammarinesi (Babboni).

The Sammarinese experience in Sandusky provides us with insights. Unable to develop their own community they joined the larger Italian community that became "home" to them. There was also a concentration of a few families on Arthur and Neal Streets, but otherwise they were scattered across the city. Another group of Sammarinesi numbering seven to eight families lived next to a quarry on Meyland Road. Within the community families took in other family members. In 1930 the Adam Berardi family in Sandusky consisted of five members along with a sister, her husband and daughter, and a lodger. Down the street Frank Grimani's family of three took in other family members and lodgers amounting to a household of nine. Neither the Italians nor the Sammarinesi had their own national church and attended the local Catholic Church.

The boardinghouse and social club experiences had a beneficial effect on the immigrants. Here they could mingle with their own people, speak the dialect, play traditional card games, celebrate religious and ethnic holidays and enjoy traditional cuisine. When they celebrated a special feast like St. Agatha day, they opened it to only Sammarinesi. They could also slowly and quietly work their way through the labyrinth of the assimilation process.

Primo Bizzocchi was one who was kind to people. In Genoa at one time he had five to six people living in their four-room apartment. Others sold coal and wood to the community when it was scarce. When Diane Uberti's father lived in New York City he even rented out the bathtub because a friend needed sleeping space and he needed money (Uberti).

Sammarinese contractors hired newly arrived immigrants. They allowed them to develop building skills and then move up the economic ladder toward the American

Dream. In Sandusky Sammarinesi became foreman and then proceeded to hire the newly arrived immigrants.

One fellow John Scali operated a Ready-Mix company and saw the value of buying acreage on the immediate outskirts of Sandusky. He divided the land into lots and sold them. Many Sammarinesi bought ready-built homes. Master bricklayer Secondo Zannoti purchased a lot and during weekends and vacations began construction of a home in 1956. With the help of friends who were in the construction business, as carpenters and tile setters they joined forces and built his home in a year.

Since 1991, the San Marino Associations have held convocations in foreign nations to interact with other Sammarinesi. For instance, in 1999 the group met in Santo Domingo in Jujuy province in Argentina.

In Detroit the Women's Auxiliary has directed the celebration of holidays, which were brought from the Old Country. On the eve of January 5 prior to the Epiphany, *La Befana* would arrive per Italian/Sammarinese folklore. She is portrayed as an old woman who delivers gifts and fills empty stockings, entering the house through the chimney similar to Santa Claus. In the past the women would celebrate with the children at the San Marino Club. The feast of St. Agatha celebrated on February 5 honors the day Pope Clement XII reestablished the sovereignty of the Republic in 1740. The day is celebrated at Sammarinese clubs with a dinner-dance and at times an official from San Marino is an honored guest. In 2002 a special play presented in the dialect was performed at a theater in Troy much to the satisfaction of all who attended.

Carnevale is celebrated as Mardi Gras is on the Tuesday before Ash Wednesday, the start of Lent. Traditional angel wings, a sweet crispy pastry made out of dough and shaped into ribbons, deep-fried and covered with powdered sugar, are made. On Tuesday evening a dinner-dance is held at the San Marino Social Club in Detroit or the San Marino Fratellanza in Queens. Dancing continues until midnight when everything ends. Another important holiday is St. Marino day, September 3 when the creation of the Republic is celebrated with a dinner-dance. On Christmas Eve there are

Fall 1978 Southgate School System. Italian lessons for children of local Sammarinese/Italian families. (They were a great bunch, and they learned quickly and well!) (Bottom Left clockwise to R) Matthew Lividini, Anita Selva, Tina Lividini, Carla Lividini, Laura Bonanni, Lea Mirella Selva, Riccardo Selva, Lisette Selva (Teacher), Anna Lividini, Jay Frucci, Marc Bonnani, Steven Selva. *Photo courtesy of Lisette Selva.*

family dinners and church attendance. Traditional *cappelletti*, a pasta stuffed with cheese is served with roast rabbit or chicken although each household does it differently (Paoletti).

In addition to maintaining their traditions the Sammarinesi encountered the process of assimilating into American life. Some of the Sammarinese who arrived immediately after World War II, were stigmatized as being attached to Italians who were seen as the former enemy during the war. The newly arrived youngsters from San Marino found it difficult to assimilate. First there was the problem of not knowing the language, which they quickly learned. American children looked down on them because they could either not speak or when they spoke English, they spoke with an accent. Nazarina Crooks who arrived in Sandusky when she was seven years old recalled that learning the language was not difficult. However once she was a teenager conditions for an immigrant became difficult. At the time it was not "hip" to be Italian or foreign and peers made fun of you (Crooks). Others like Carlo Dall'Olmo found that they were "sad, lonely, miserable" in the new society without their friends and relatives left behind in San Marino. Holidays like Christmas were celebrated differently.

Rise of the Second Generation

The Sammarinese immigrants who came to the United States assimilated, maintained their heritage, and thrived at their jobs. They watched as their children dealt with American society and hopeful that they would emulate their success. They were not to be disappointed.

An earlier second-generation success story was that of Anthony Guerra who eventually became owner of LEWCO (Lake Erie Welding Company). His father Joseph was born in San Marino immigrated to the United States in 1927 and worked along with his brothers as a laborer at a stone quarry in Sandusky. Anthony was born in 1932 and served in the Korean War where he was trained as a welder.

In Sandusky, LEWCO started in 1917 as the Ohio Welding Company that welded and sold welding supplies and medical gases. Then in 1952, the Grumney brothers bought the plant and renamed it Lake Erie Welding and Fabricating. At the time the factory had four employees and then decided to hire a fifth welder, Tony Guerra fresh out of the U.S. Navy. Eight years later Tony bought into the business as a 50 percent partner and by 1973 was the sole owner of the company, expanded it and renamed it, LEWCO.

In a few instances some Sammarinese-Americans married African Americans. There was a mixed response from the parents and the community. Some had no problems if the spouse was of the same social class and shared similar values (Crooks).

In the early days the Sammarinesi helped each other and worked together. Boys like Gabriele Bugli worked for their dads as young as eight years of age. As a teenager he worked all summer for his father. He learned the cement trade in all its aspects. Other children succeeded working in factories, construction, or were self-employed. With hard work, the possibilities were unlimited.

The role of education of their children depended on the father and his view of the American experience. Some of them were so tied to their Sammarinese traditions, that they saw no need for college education for women. What these individuals did not realize was that their daughters were not realizing their potential or the fact that a higher education would result in better pay (Crooks).

For many, education was an important step to enter the professions and white collar jobs, where many have succeeded. What follows are a number of Sammarinesi and Sammarinese-Americans who have developed in this niche. In Michigan, New York, and Sandusky the second generation has entered the professions. They are found as teachers from kindergarten through college, in law, architecture, civil engineering, medicine, pharmacy, dentistry, and business. A bit of advice by an immigrant, which had its effect was "it is easier to push a pencil than to push a shovel full of cement" (Dall'Olmo).

Two immigrants to enter the professions were Livio Capicchioni and Carlo Dall'Olmo. Mr. Capicchioni (1928-2001) arrived in Detroit as a surveyor. Inspired by the Government Palace in San Marino he designed the San Marino Social Club in 1975, which remains a landmark on Big Beaver Road in Troy, Michigan.

The first Sammarinese immigrant to receive a medical degree was Carlo Dall'Olmo. He had to work hard as an immigrant student "to prove himself." He obtained a medical degree (M.D.) from Wayne State University School of Medicine. His specialty is vascular surgery with an office in Flint. He is affiliated with multiple hospitals in the area including the Genesys Regional Medical Center and Hurley Medical Center. Following his passion to help people Dr.

Dall'Olmo has volunteered his time on several occasions to travel to Landstuhl Regional Medical Center in Germany operated by the U.S. Army and the Department of Defense. Here he worked on soldiers, who had been seriously injured while serving in Afghanistan.

Other physicians include Dr. Joseph Uberti who received a Ph.D. (1979) and M.D. (1983) from Wayne State University School of Medicine. He is an oncologist specializing in bone marrow transplant and is associated with the Barbara Ann Karmanos Cancer Institute in Detroit, the largest cancer research and provider network in Michigan. Dr. Dennis Giannini received his M.D. from Wayne State University School of Medicine in 1985. Based in Troy, Michigan this physiatrist focuses on chronic pain, prosthetics, surgery recovery, nerve damage, sports medicine, and rehabilitation.

Dr. Gabriele G. Bugli took a turn at cement work and then decided to attend the University of Michigan graduating in 1983. Now he operates out of Family Dental Care in the Detroit suburb of Sterling Heights. On the other hand his brother Marco received a degree in mechanical engineering but decided to go into cement work and bought into his father's company, Metropolitan Construction (Bugli).

Dr. Marc Bonanni DPM is a practicing Podiatrist (foot specialist) in Dexter, Michigan. He graduated from William M. Scholl College of Podiatric Medicine at the Rosalind Franklin University of Medicine in 1997. He is affiliated with hospitals in the Ann Arbor area.

In metro New York Dr. Enrico M. Ligniti (Pham D, MSCP) is assistant professor of pediatrics at Hofstra-Northwell School of Medicine; director, pediatric pharmacy service line for Northwell Health; and director of pediatric pharmacy services at Cohen Children's Medical Center. He received his pharmacy education at St. John's University and Duquesne University.

Across the continent, James Bizzochi, a graduate of Massachusetts Institute of Technology with a Master of Science degree in Comparative Media Studies, teaches at Simon Fraser University's School of Interactive Art and Technology in Vancouver, British Columbia. He is a documentary filmmaker and video artist whose ability has been recognized by awards.

In the field of business Paul Calmi, a graduate of Walsh College in accounting, has led a successful career as a CPA in Sterling Heights. He is the chief financial officer at Casadei Steel Inc. and is connected as a CPA with Godfrey Hammel, Danneals & Company.

World Trade Center Disaster

A citizen of the tiny Republic of San Marino was a victim of the World Trade Center disaster of September 11, 2001. Steven A. Giorgetti (1957-2001), was the son of Sammarinese immigrants, Luigi and Anna Giorgetti.

Steven worked for Marsh & McLennan for 20 years. Marsh & McLennan is a global professional services firm headquartered in mid-town New York City, with businesses in insurance brokerage, risk management, reinsurance services, talent management, reinvestment advisory, and management consulting. Today it is considered one of the world's largest insurance brokers.

In September 2001 Mr. Giorgetti had been nominated for a promotion to managing director. He worked at the company's mid-town offices but was at the World Trade Center for a meeting on September 11. He was on the 90th floor in the north tower when the jet struck. The promotion was given to him posthumously.

As the *New York Times* wrote he was "dashing, hard-working and unfailingly in a good mood, he worked his way up to senior vice president. And beyond."

Mr. Giorgetti, his wife Arminé of 18 years and two children lived in Manhasset on Long Island. "On a rare occasion he had to miss one of his son's Little League games for a business dinner, Mr. Giorgetti telephoned his wife not once but three times, asking for updates. His daughter was his princess. Mr. Giorgetti decorated his home office with pictures of Joe DiMaggio and Mickey Mantle. At work, his office was unmistakably that of a Daddy, adorned with arts and crafts projects galore." He is buried on the site at the National September 11 Memorial (*New York Times* 12-30-2001).

Women

In the Old Country life for women was not easy, especially in a male dominated society. Young women had to sell eggs in order to obtain a dowry. They did their laundry in pools of running water. During the winter when the temperature grew frigid the women had to break the ice in order to wash their laundry. They returned home with baskets of clean clothing, but their fingers were cut and bleeding from the ordeal. Obviously for many young girls education was out of the question. Many Sammarinese immigrant women are listed in the Ellis Island immigration records as illiterate.

In 1947, children were sent off to farms to do their "apprenticeship" in return for food and shelter, but they could not leave the farm. Appalled by this mistreatment to children Stella Capicchioni, a teacher, protested their child abuse to the government. She felt that children should not have to be "rented out" for the family to survive (Uberti and Capicchioni).

We can view the role of Sammarinese women across the United States. The majority of women remained at home as housewives to care for their children. Where land was available close to home women maintained large gardens in rural places like Kelleys Island augmenting their family's diet with fresh vegetables. The women also kept small animals like chickens and had a supply of eggs and eventually an old hen for the soup pot. Where possible some of them had cows, which provided the family with dairy products and the surplus sold to neighbors.

Kelleys Island was in the heartland of grape growing and wine making. Annually in September, the vineyard owners would put out a call for the Sammarinesi and other women to come and pick the grapes that would be processed into wine.

The women who arrived from San Marino came either as wives with their husbands, to join them, or as prospective brides. Newly arrived women found learning English a challenge, not experienced by their husbands because the men were in the labor force and had to learn English. Naturally the Sammarinese dialect was spoken at home. Besides speaking the dialect at home and Italian with Italian women, they could find an Italian speaking grocer if they were fortunate or made themselves understood through gestures.

The biggest commercial activity Sammarinese women got involved with was operating a boardinghouse. As we have seen earlier the first Sammarinese female in the United States, Tina Lombardi Renganeschi, opened a boardinghouse – Albergo Titano – in Greenwich Village and worked in the family restaurant. Following this tradition Sammarinese widows or housewives rented out rooms usually to Sammarinesi and other boarders "just off the boat." The first roomers in Detroit paid $5 per week and this rose to $10-$15 weekly for room and board. To add to the monthly revenue for room and board they sold homemade wine at 10 cents a glass and this was a big revenue getter. The boarding house experience provided the family with important supplemental income, at times rivaling the head of the house's income (Umberti).

For an immigrant's insights into the boardinghouse experience, we can tap the reminiscences of Giancarlo Ferri (1935-2011) who lived in Elmont, New York between December 1954 and September 1955. When he arrived in the United States at nineteen years of age he lived in a boarding house. Being a foreigner to the area, he was happy to find that in a three to four block area there were many Sammarinese households. Maria kept the boardinghouse and provided home-cooked meals reminiscent of what he had eaten at home. After dinner the group of immigrant boarders would sit around and discuss the day's activities and talk about problems they faced in American society (Ferri).

In the Old Country women developed lace making and embroidery as a cottage industry and sewed clothing for themselves and family. When they came to the United States, they found employment as seamstresses or entered the dressmaking business. As private seamstresses they brought mending projects to their home, worked on their own account, and all the while continued to oversee their families. Luigina Silvagni Ciavatta originally from Serraville, owned and operated a tailor shop with her husband, Dino, at Niagara Falls, New York until her death in 2003 at 82 years of age. In some instances Sammarinesi moved east to the Big Apple from Sandusky and even Detroit because they saw greater job opportunity (Paoletti). In 1930, Mary Bucci was a seamstress working for a wholesale women's clothing factory in Detroit. Marina Mavassi in 1940 living in the Bronx was a finisher of women's wear. At the same time in NYC Antonia Burgagni was working as a dressmaker in a shop. Stella Zonzini born in Serraville and came to the United States in 1958 was an accomplished seamstress well known for fashion design and excelled in workmanship. It is important to note that seamstresses could utilize this type of skilled labor to make fairly good wages either out of the home or in a sewing shop.

Other women found employment in local industries in large cities. One woman worked at a Sandusky factory making radios and refrigerators, but soon found that there was plenty of work at home as children came along. Many Sammarinese women in Sandusky found employment at Clay Products that produced a variety of ceramic items including electrical insulators. Then there was 20-year-old Rose Muratori working as a laborer in a Sandusky rubber factory while another woman, Mary Muratori was a shipping packer.

Sammarinese women got hospital jobs, were employed as domestic servants, while a number became teachers. Amelia Casadei (1917-2001) opened a beauty salon, which was a service business that had an immediate impact with customers who sought beauty treatments. Women entered the restaurant business. Deo and Maria De Biagi operated a liquor store on New York's Third Avenue. For many years from the 1940s on, Eurosia Berardi known to all as "Momma Berardi" sold her famous French fries at Cedar Point Amusement Park in Sandusky. She was aided by Mary Capicchioni, the first female to be employed by the Berardis in 1942 as a pre-teen. In Detroit, Pia Malpeli was a sewing machine operator for the Carhartt Clothing Company.

A number of female immigrants married outside the Sammarinese world and ended up in areas far from Sammarinese centers. We have Catarina Canton married to an Italian farmer in western Montana's Ravalli County who was kept busy with farm tasks and keeping house. Jean, a Sammarinese woman, married Dr. Thomas Hutton and in 1940 was living in Spalding in Menominee County in Michigan's Upper Peninsula.

By the 21st century we find Sammarinese-American women in law, real estate, massotherapy, restaurateuring, teaching, business to name a few fields of endeavor. In Sandusky, Joanne Berardi is a prominent realtor and Maria Berardi is both a massage therapist and restaurant owner.

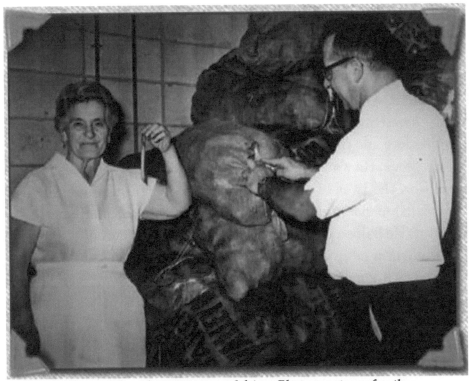

"Momma Berardi" with potatoes and fries. *Photo courtesy of author.*

Politics, Sports, Religion, & Culture

Politics

In general the Sammarinesi usually did not get involved in local and state politics, but there are instances of them involved on the township level (Putti). One individual was Nello Bianchi (1923-2007). His father, Adamo, immigrated to Kelleys Island in 1928 sponsored by his brother-in-law and was followed a year later by his wife and five-year old son, Nello. He grew up on Kelleys Island and helped support the family at 16 years of age. He went on to serve in World War II and returned to the islands afterwards.

Nello was appointed postmaster of Put-in-Bay, Ohio in 1966 and served for 25 years; he had a 20-year term on the fire department; served seven terms on the board of education; and three terms on the Put-in-Bay Township board of trustees. He was community spirited and actively sought to improve the lives of people. He was instrumental in building a township hall and garage, a new fire station and senior center. He helped create a Port Authority and secured funding to build and maintain island airports. Upon his death he was hailed as a long-time public servant.[33]

An interesting Sammarinese-American politician is Frank Valli. His father, Marino Valli, was born in Pergamino, Argentina and emigrated to Sandusky, Ohio. His son Frank was born in 1929 and after graduating from Sandusky High School he went to Bowling Green State University where he played football. He graduated in 1952 with a degree in business administration and then served in the Korean War. Upon his return from the war he developed a bail bond agency, which was tied into the Frank M. Valli Agency dealing with real estate and insurance. He was elected Vice Director of Professional Bail Agents of the United States and was named bail bondsman of the year in 2001.

In the 1960s and 1970s he ran for the city commission and as a Democratic state representative for Erie County, losing both elections. Then in 1995 he was elected to the Sandusky city commission, where he played an active role and was re-elected in 1998 and subsequent years. In a way, Valli said being a commissioner was like poker games he liked to play with his buddies. "You never know what hand you are going to get." He served as vice mayor for two years and later was the ex-officio mayor in 2002. Valli at 89 years of age continued to be involved in his businesses.[34]

Out West, Peter Bugli was involved in the local communities of the Bitter Root Valley, south of Missoula, Montana. In the 1940s he served in a number of official positions on the Ravalli County Pomona Grange and in 1950 he was president of the Florence Carlton Grange when it was established. The local Democratic party put his name up to run for Ravalli County sheriff. He lost the race to unseat the incumbent sheriff.[35]

In a unique development there are three individuals who were born in the United States who play important roles in Sammarinese life. A Sammarinese politician, Rosa Zafferoni was born in Jersey City, New Jersey on August 16, 1960. She was a member of the Sammarinese Christian Democratic Party until she left with the rest of the left-wing faction of the party to form the Center Democrats. She has served as Secretary of State for health, education and interior and twice as a Captain Regent (April-October 1999 and 2008). Kristina Paradalos was born in New York City (10-14-1973) served as a judge in San Marino and currently is a judge of the European Court of Human Rights.

HAVE A CHANGE IN THE SHERIFF'S OFFICE

Elect

PETER BUGLI

Democrat For

SHERIFF

**For Honest, Efficient, and Courteous Service
I Will Do My Best to Serve You Well**

I am just completing a canvass of the entire county. I have tried to call upon everyone but it is a big job and I know I have missed many people who I would have liked to meet to present myself as a candidate for sheriff. On Nov. 7th I trust everyone will get out and vote in order to elect the candidates who you consider most likely to provide our families with the best government possible. I hope you will give careful consideration to my candidacy.

If elected Sheriff of Ravalli County I will do my best to enforce the laws of the State of Montana and for the interests of Ravalli County.

Sincerely yours,

PETE BUGLI

Circ. and Paid for By Peter Bugli

Sports

Various sports played a role in the lives of the immigrants. One activity San Marino is traditionally known for promoting is the use of the mediaeval cross bow, which some might consider the national sport. The Crossbow Corps is a volunteer group within the Sammarinese Army and is a ceremonial force of around seventy soldiers. However, in the United States few individuals have been interested in pursuing this traditional activity (Babboni).

A traditional sport among the Sammarinesi is bocce/bocci, a ball sport closely related to British bowls. It is played at clubs on a regular basis by both men and women. The Italian-American Bocce Auxiliary has sponsored a field of sixteen teams at its annual Bocce Rama tournament held at the club. A noted player in Sandusky, Ohio was Pierina Zanotti who played on the Italian-American Beneficial Club and Ladies Auxiliary team. She served as captain of her squad and won numerous championships over the years.[36] As Frank Valli said in 1995 at the Italian-American Social Club in Sandusky, "You can be 85 and have crutches and still play this game."

Until the latter half of the twentieth century soccer has not been a popular sport in the United States, especially among children. With the arrival of Sammarinese immigrants after World War II many were soccer players who had played for national teams. As a result, they promoted soccer locally. When the San Marino Social Club opened in 1975 it included a regulation soccer field. In 1981 the San Marino Soccer

Sports Club was established. From a single soccer team, it has expanded to include members of all ages.

Between 1981 and 1987 the Sports Club sponsored teams but have achieved success in the international field as well. The men's-over-30 soccer team won the first "Michigan Cup" game in Michigan and Canada. The young men's less-than-19 soccer team toured England and competed in a 1986 tournament in Aberdeen, Scotland. The skill of the soccer players has been recognized by having a San Marino player selected as the "Most Valuable Player" in the Aberdeen tournament. Several players from the soccer teams have been selected to represent Michigan in multi-state tournament play.

In 2005 the soccer team was composed of club members and people from neighboring communities. The Sammarinesi were the catalyst for the popularity of soccer. Today the field is rented out to local youth soccer groups in surrounding Troy. In recent years the San Marino Soccer Club continues to flourish. It has participated in the Gerhard Mengel State Cup and the Italian-American Champion Cup. So it is safe to say that the Sammarinesi were the catalyst for the popularity of soccer in north Metro Detroit.

In an unusual development, William Marino Guerra was born in Detroit in 1968 and was a former soccer/football player who played international soccer for San Marino and Italy as a defender. After graduating from the San Marino youth set-up he made appearances for San Marino national football: two in 1987 before joining FIFA and 38 FIFA sanctioned games between 1990 and 1999. He is the republic's tenth most-capped player of all times. Also he captained the San Marino team on five occasions between 1995 and 1997. He retired in 2004 at age 36. When not in the field he was a house painter and decorator.

One of the most famous of sportsmen among the Michigan Sammarinesi was the bicyclist, Fernando Capicchioni also known as Fred Cappy. He was born in Fiorentino, San Marino in 1912 and became involved in bicycle racing in France in 1928 where he first emigrated to work. A year later he immigrated to the United States and briefly settled in Detroit before moving to New York City where he became involved in racing with the *Unione Sportiva Italiana*. In 1932 he qualified for the Los Angeles Olympics but had the admission rescinded because he was not an American citizen. When the Italian cycling team trained in New York City, Capicchioni beat Attilio Pavesi who later won a gold medal.

In March 1936 he was in Detroit where he won the cup in the Amateur Six Day race held in the old velodrome. He also took part in a professional six-day race in August where he finished fifth and lost any chance to race in the Olympics. In 1937 he met racer John Barbieri and they both decided that Detroit needed added pep to its cycling program. They started the East Side Wheelmen Club and registered all riders with the Amateur Bicyclist League of America. Cappy's tireless efforts as organizer and promoter injected life into the sport. Although he had become a pro he did so much for amateur cycling in Detroit upon his return that American Bicycling League reinstated him as an amateur in 1937. He cycled his last race in 1941 winning the East Side Wheelmen Club championship on a track at Morang and Harper in Detroit.

In 1937 Capicchioni started the "Fred Cappy Bicycle Trophy Race, which continued even after he left Detroit in 1979. In 1969 Cappy and Mike Walden successfully built the Dorais Velodrome at Mound Road and Outer Drive. As a result the national championships were held in Detroit, the first time since 1940. The velodrome operated from 1969 until 1989 and today remains abandoned with uncertain plans for the future.

By 1973 Cappy had been named "Mr. Bicycle" by the *Belgian News* and was promoting amateur cycling as an administrator and sponsor of "The Cappy Classic" considered one of the best races in the United States. On November 21 Cappy was inducted into the Michigan Amateur Sports Hall of Fame. In 1988 Cappy, the US Cycling Federation director, became a lifetime member of the federation. Three years later he was inducted into the U.S. Bicycling Hall of Fame in Somerville, New Jersey and he was also inducted into the Olympic Hall of Fame in Cycling.

In 1979 he left Detroit for Colorado Spring where he and his wife Mary directed and guided the U.S. Cycling Federation. They raised funding from $50,000 to over $700,000 and increased membership from 18,000 to 25,000. During the 1984 Los Angeles Olympics the United States won numerous medals in all categories due to the efforts of the Capicchionis. In 1984 Mary died and two years later a new cycling track was inaugurated honoring both Mary and Fred Cappy. When he died in 1999 Fernando Capicchioni was seen as a major force in the development of bicycle racing in Metro Detroit.[37]

The Cappy bicycling legacy is alive at the Lexus Velodrome in mid-town Detroit, the second indoor velodrome in the United States, opened in January 2018. The $ 4 million cost was paid for by an undisclosed "angel donor" and is operated by the nonprofit Detroit Fitness Foundation established in 2016.[38]

Cappy also proved to be a good bowler. He began bowling in 1942 as a southpaw. Three years later with an average of 176 he was rolling for three leagues. He participated in the International Lefthander's Tournament as well.

Some of the Sammarinesi got into a variety of sports, not frequented by many nationalities. One of these was ice racing or ice yachting on the frozen waters of Sandusky Bay. It began when a couple of boys had iceboats on Kelleys Island as the conditions around the islands off Sandusky were ideal for ice racing. Anthony Moscioni got interested in the sport and as he got older he built his own iceboat. A member of the Ice Yacht Club, he was an amateur sailor and used to enjoy having a good time of it. Moscioni won a few local races and traveled to Mount Clemens, Michigan and other local lake-communities for competitions. However he had to admit that they were amateurs and that national races were dominated by a strong competition. Traveling to races was risky because it took time and was costly and once you arrived the race could be cancelled due to bad weather and/ice conditions. Mosconi raced until the early 1970s. Louie Estralla lived in Frankfort and had a thirty-foot ice yacht that he raced on Lake Michigan (Babboni).

Dino Crescentini was a quality builder and had the time, energy, and finances to enter the fast world of racing cars and bobsleds. He began his career in auto racing in San Marino, before he left for the United States, when his parents gave him a 850 Fiat Coupé. Speed was his passion and the hilly nature of San Marino provided the necessary thrills. After he emigrated he was too busy getting settled to worry much about auto racing. However in 1978 he went to a Formula One Grand Prix in Canada and the old lure of racing re-attracted him. After the necessary training, Crescentini received his racing license and he was on the speedway again. He raced on and off until 1989 when he gave it up. Some six years later he picked up racing again. Dino loved speed and auto racing and he continued to race.

After Jean-Pierre Renzi saw what the Jamaican bobsled team did at the 1988 Winter Olympics for their island nation, maybe a bobsled with the Republic of San Marino's colors could take to the slopes at the 1994 Winter Olympics in Lillehammer, Norway. Knowing that Dino had a passion for speed, Renzi approached him. At first, he was a bit skeptical given his age, but they decided to form a team. When Renzi dropped out, Dino formed a team with two others, his brother Joe and Michael Crocenci. They found it difficult to rent a bobsled. When they found one, they had to repair it to their satisfaction, and then had to travel to Lake Placid, New York where they could train. After a number of poor bobsleds they bought their own. Although the Club and others donated money, they were basically on their own. When they went to Lillehammer they had not trained for 25 days. However the days of the race, out of fifty-one nations competing, they finished 39th. As Dino reminisced, "if they had more luck and more training they might have done better." However they did bring some quick fame to the Republic when the bobsled came down the track with the blue and white national colors. Since the Winter Olympics are now every two years, there was some talk that Dino would reconstitute the team, but the others lost interest and that was the end of San Marino's time with the bobsled.

Crescentini returned to racing in 1995 having done so much of it in his life. As his wife Vincenzina said, "he was a gorgeous, caring man who just loved life and all racing." She was never able to get him to abandon racing. On June 22, 2008 he was killed at Mosport International Raceway near Bowmanville, Ontario, in a violent high-speed vintage car racing accident.[39]

Another sports figure is Matthew "Matt" Capiccioni, whose grandfather was from San Marino and thus he holds dual citizenship. He was born in Brecksville, Ohio, a suburb of Greater Cleveland in 1980. He attended Cleveland State University and received a Bachelor of Arts in communications. For ten years he was involved with competitive gymnastics and in 1999 he won gold medals in both the rings and the vault at AAU Junior Olympic Games. Between 1999 and 2001 he trained at the Cleveland Pro-Wrestling Training School and then joined the professional wrestling circuit. Some of his ring names: Matt Cross, The 18th Amendment, M-Dogg 20, and Son of Havoc. He is also known for leading a straight-edge life style (no drugs nor alcohol). He was featured in Series 6 of American Ninja Warrior, but did not qualify. He also appeared in the video game, "Backyard Wresting: Don't Try this at Home." In 2017 Capiccioni started the clothing company, Wrestling Is Forever.

In high school and college numerous Sammarinese-Americans got involved in a variety of sports. In an era when being "foreign" was not "in" with kids, sports were a means to Americanization. This was especially true in baseball and football, but other sports followed like ice hockey.

Hunting carried on in the Old Country was limited to birds: pheasants, woodpeckers, blackbirds, and ducks and rabbits. As Walter Babboni said, "In San Marino if it had feathers they shot it." Men and women worked together with large trap bags into which they drove literally thousands of blackbirds over the years. The birds were cleaned and plucked usually by children. The birds were filled with rosemary, garlic and sage and salt pork was added then they were sauté in pan until cooked. Many times wine was added when almost done and the birds were served as an entrée.[40]

Avid hunters of small game and deer brought this tradition to the United States. Babboni's father and father-in-law were excellent hunters. The kids grew up with wild game as a table staple. During the Depression of the 1930s and later the Sammarinesi did not just hunt for adventure but hunted to stock their food larders or give the excess away nothing was wasted. Some of the immigrants hunted pheasants on the outskirts of Warren and into Clinton Township, Michigan in the 1930s where they were plentiful. Over the years others traveled farther north and even into the Upper Peninsula to hunt for pheasants and other game (Babboni).

A related sport was skeet shooting. Anyone interested and qualified joined a group who headed for the skeet range. Three to four hours were spent shooting. Many members of the San Marino Club enjoyed skeet shooting and small game hunting (Calmi).

A group of Sammarinese hunters almost landed in federal court due to their hunting enthusiasm. As Secondo Zanotti recounted in the vicinity of Sandusky a group of bird hunters approached fenced federal government property. Suddenly pheasants were going under and over the fence. They pulled up the fence and trespassed and quickly shot 5-6 birds as a security siren went off and a military policeman intervened. He seized their guns and they thought they were destined for federal court in Toledo and possibly a fine or even a jail term. Due to a friend, the commanding officer who understood what they were doing had their guns returned and they were not charged with trespassing.

The waters around Michigan attracted Sammarinesi who would fish primarily for fun and not necessarily to bring home large amounts of fish. Secondo Zanotti became an avid fisherman and with friends fished the island-bound waters off Sandusky. When he arrived from San Marino he recalled that leafless trees and frozen Lake Erie reminded him of what he knew about Alaska and remained indoors during the winter. One day in 1953 he was crossing a bridge on Sandusky Bay and saw people ice fishing. He quickly learned how to fish in an ice shanty and developed a new winter activity. In the early years they brought back sacks of fish caught in Sandusky Bay but by the 1990s the catch had drastically declined. Secondo was proud of the fact that in

1993 he caught an award winning 33-inch walleye weighing twelve pounds. Sammarinesi vacationing in Key West, Florida returned home with coolers full of fish. The United States proved to be a virtual hunting and fishing paradise for these Sammarinesi whose homeland was limited for these activities.[41]

Religion

The vast majority of Sammarinesi have retained their Roman Catholic faith. This was especially true of the first and second generations of immigrants and their children. Given their small numbers in the three communities, a "Little San Marino" never arose, which could have included a Sammarinese Catholic Church as was so common among the much larger Italian population.

In Detroit's Little Italy on Gratiot Street many attended San Francesco and Holy Family (Italian) Catholic churches, but others attended the nearest Catholic Church in the neighborhood. In the Oakwood-Fort Street community they were served by Our Lady of Mt. Carmel Catholic church, which catered to an Italian congregation. In Elmont, there is St. Boniface Catholic church for the immigrants and their children. This continues as they have moved into the suburbs. However, today some continue to frequent San Francesco church, which has moved with the Italian-American population to Clinton Township. Some serve as lay leaders and on parish councils in their respective parishes or are involved Catholic education. However as later generations of Sammarinesi intermarry with other nationalities and religions it becomes ever more difficult to maintain such a strong religious identity.

Cultural Maintenance

For a small immigrant group, the Sammarinesi are adamant in preserving their culture and heritage "through [celebration of] religious feast days, remembrance of San Marino, food, dancing, folklore, card playing, and special dishes for different occasions." The immigrants and their children find Italian magazines, newspapers, and DVDs for music especially through Bonaldi's Book Store in Clinton Township (Capicchioni).

Organizations

By the 1930s there were enough Sammarinesi in New York City and Detroit to contemplate the development of social-fraternal-heritage organizations. In 1935 seven Sammarinesi met in New York City and formed the *Fratellanza Sammarinese di New York* (Sammarinese Brotherhood of New York), which was formally established soon after. Its purpose was to maintain and strengthen the heritage, traditions, and pride of the mother country and to organize events to perpetuate these ideas. On February 4, 1940, a day before the feast of St. Agatha, patron of San Marino, the Central Opera House was the site for the grand ball celebration of the Bicentennial of the Reconquest of Liberty of the Republic of San Marino. They also celebrated the founding of the Fratellanza. Over the years the Fratellanza continues to have dances, banquets, and musical concerts promoting Sammarinese culture. The 4th of July is celebrated at Lido Beach, Long Island. The major festivals that were celebrated: the arrival of *La Befana* at Christmas time, Flavors of the Past, and the feast of Saint Agatha (February 5).

From the beginning the Sammarinese immigrants in Detroit always got together on weekends, especially in the summertime. They went to a picnic ground at Nine Mile and Jefferson where they had picnics and played cards, especially the Italians game of *morra*. The Sammarinesi saw that the Lombardi and Veneti had their own mutual beneficial societies. During the first years the Sammarinesi rented either of these halls for their events. Having seen how successful these other societies were they began to dream of forming their own mutual beneficial society. Not only would the club provide benefits, but it would also provide them with a focal point for their interest in their heritage and the Old Country.

Once the Sammarinesi in Detroit heard of the progress of their New York countrymen they decided to establish their own club. One of the first organizational meetings with a dozen men took place in Primo Bizzocchi's kitchen around the large kitchen table. Three of the founding members were: Ferucco Amati, Martin Bucci, and David Zaffarani. Amati and Zaffarani were tile setters and Bucci was a successful automobile repairman (Uberti).

The Detroit Sammarinesi established their club on February 6, 1938 (within a day of the feast day of St. Agatha). The founders wrote their goals and aspirations of the club at the first meeting:

We emigrants of the Republic of San Marino, residing in Detroit, Michigan, have formed a Society to help each other and to preserve, in a foreign land, the old traditions of the Republic of San Marino. To meet, once a month, as one family, all the Sammarinesi, and their sons, residing in the city of Detroit, Michigan and bordering cities, whose priority is friendship, respect of others' political and religious opinions, and to improve their moral and material standards, in benevolence, harmony, and brotherhood.

The club was typical of mutual beneficial clubs and offered benefits for the sick. The club proved to be an immediate success as the community now had a place to meet, socialize, and relive life in the Old Country. For new immigrants it provided a "secure base" where they could gradually assimilate into American society. The Club promoted Sammarinese heritage, which was appreciated by the immigrants. The Club had approximately 350 members out of several thousand Sammarinesi in Metro Detroit (Bugli).

Between the foundation of the club and 1954 the members met in a variety of locations in homes and basements. Having seen how successful other clubs were, a group of Sammarinesi decided to build their own structure. Weren't most of the members in construction? They constructed their first building at 11350 E. McNichols Road. This project was not started without a certain amount of apprehension, due to concerns over uncertainty and diversity of opinion. When the first clubhouse was inaugurated in 1955 Governor "Soapy" Williams attended the event.

As the Sammarinese immigrants and their children moved into the suburbs, members of the club decided to move to Big Beaver Road in Troy. Livio Capicchioni, an architect with Michael S. Downs & Associates of Oak Park, and Sebastiano Casadei created the structure's design reminiscent of the Government Palace in the mother country.

Governor "Soapy" Williams at San Marino Club. *Photo courtesy of author.*

It was financed by members and aided by their volunteering time in the construction process. It was dedicated on October 24, 1976. The three-acre site includes the Sammarinese cultural center with its spacious halls, recreation field, and Club House. Here you find the banquet facilities; the office of the San Marino Consulate of Detroit; and the office of the Comunità Sammarinese di Detroit. It remains a popular site for weddings and banquets. The San Marino Club has dinners and dances honoring San Marino/St. Marinus in September 3 celebrating the foundation of the Republic of San Marino and St. Agatha on February 5 celebrating the return of Sammarinese autonomy and freedom from Cardinal Alberoni's invasion on February 5, 1740. In the early days the annual picnic was held at Venetian Park at 13 Mile near Gratiot where a band provided dance music. Everyone brought a dish, which was passed around and as Walter Babboni concluded "it was fun" as this small group of immigrants could visit and enjoy each other's company.

As opposed to, unfortunately, many ethnic clubs, the San Marino Club has a high percent of active members - 100 out of 200. Events on Saturday and Sunday evenings attract 40-50 people. Card parties and weddings also attract many family members and members (Calmi).

San Marino Club, Troy, Michigan. *Courtesy of sanmarinoclub.com*

The San Marino Social Club developed a restaurant and catering business in Troy known as Tre Monti. For decades it was renowned throughout North Detroit and Clinton Township for its delicious cuisine. In 2018 the restaurant was closed and was replaced by Cantoro Italian Trattoria, which remained in business on site for a year. Today the San Marino Banquet Hall caters to weddings, corporate events, and a variety of occasions.

In the Detroit area there are other clubs and organizations dedicated to assisting the Sammarinesi retain their heritage and ties to the Old Country. The San Marino Ladies' Auxiliary was founded in June 1975. Its purpose is to sustain moral support for the male members of the San Marino Social Club and to constitute a society of friendship and entertainment. On the entertainment front the auxiliary has Halloween and Christmas parties for children, prepares the annual Social Club picnics, and has held the Miss San Marino Pageant. Over the years the members have sponsored various activities that have raised funds for various charities. They have contributed to Leukemia Research Life, Make-A-Wish Foundation, American Cancer Society, Christmas food baskets, and numerous local charities. Furthermore, they provide the Social Club with an annual donation and oversee ethnic celebrations during the year.

The Sammarinese Community of Detroit (*Comunità Sammarinese di Detroit*) was established on March 3, 1980 and is sponsored by the Republic. With 1,228 members it is the largest of the 25 similar organizations around the world. It is an important association, which unites local communities with the Old Country, promotes scholarships, and social events. Representatives of the organization meet annually in San Marino with government officials to discuss the concerns and to maintain the right to vote in the homeland. It has been a tight knit group of immigrants who sought to maintain contact with the political and economic life of San Marino. It unites local communities with the Old Country, promotes scholarships, and social events.

In Sandusky as we have seen there was never a large population to create separate institutions. The Italian America Beneficial Club became home to the Sammarinese community. The organization was helpful in assimilating the immigrants. Even with this club the Sammarinesi remained ethnically united and never totally lost their culture to the Italians. They would attend club dances and picnics. However for special Sammarinese days like the celebration of the feast of St. Agatha (February 5) or San Marino (September 3) they rented rooms at the club but did not invite the Italians. In the summer the Sammarinesi hold their own picnic. The picnic centers around sausage al la San Marino served with peppers and covered dishes that everyone brings. There are games for children and the adults play *tombola* similar to bingo. They also use the time to bring photos and reminiscence about life in San Marino and share news from the Old Country. It is one of the biggest events of the year for Sammarinesi. Coming from this tiny nation they have been adamant that they maintain their identity and heritage (Zanotti).

The Sammarinesi are concerned with the common goal of maintaining family ties and upholding tradition and see the future of the San Marino Club in the hands of the youth. To maintain a cohesive connection between the homeland and the youth, the *Soggiorni Culturali* (Cultural Subjects) has been held since the summer of 1980. A selected number of students from various Sammarinese clubs are sent to the Republic of San Marino. They spend three weeks there learning the culture, history, and language of the country along with young people from Argentina, France, England, Canada, and other parts of the United States. In Michigan the publication *The Young Sammarinese* was first published on April 8, 1975. Seven years later the Young Sammarinese Club was organized to bring young people together in order to socialize and share their culture.

For adults a number of organizations of trans-Atlantic concern have been established. In 1978 the Sammarinese Association of the Fratellanza San Marino-America was established. A thousand members formed the group, which links America with the Old Country. New York-based ASER (San Marino Equal Rights Association) was established to promote Sammarinese citizenship and equal rights.

Theater, Music, Art, & Cinema

Over the years the Sammarinesi developed their own culture in Michigan and other states. Early theater developed in the Detroit Sammarinese community and local plays were performed. Ferucco Amati was a wonderful comedian and a riot on stage. They also performed serious plays. Mother Amati was involved and rehearsed at home. There were also Sicilian and Russian Jewish immigrants involved in their performances. Although these plays came to an end years ago, the tradition continues in a modified form. In the Fall of 2002, the *Comedia* from San Marino visited the Detroit area and

Fall 1981, San Marino art & history exhibit, Sterling Heights, Michigan. Carla Selva. The lovely medieval dress was sewn by Sammarinese seamstress Maria Bucci. The exhibit featured beautiful ceramics, paintings, musical instruments, (a famed violin) and a handmade crossbow, among other things. *Photo courtesy of Lisette Selva*

put on a play dealing with the immigrant story and presented it in the Sammarinese dialect. Many in the audience were enthralled by this performance and a return to former times (Amati).

Various Sammarinesi have played roles in the field of music and art. Giovanni (Gianni) de Biagi (1925-2004) was one of these musicians who was born in San Marino where he learned his basic musical skills before immigrating to the United States. He completed his academic preparation at Columbia and Long Island Universities and then trained with numerous piano artists. He performed throughout the United States and in Montréal, Québec and had radio performances. In New York and Florida he frequently lectured on the life and works of Giuseppe Verdi, Frederic Chopin, and the development of Maurice Ravel's *Bolero*. He taught at the Island Tree Schools (1968-1989) and made a deep impression on the students he taught, giving them an appreciation of music and theater.

Biagi received numerous awards for his work as a musician and educator. His last performance was appropriately held at the Ellis Island Immigration Museum in 2001 at the request of the San Marino government for the opening of the exhibit, "A Small State in the Great History – San Marino Emigration."[42]

Riccardo Selva was born in Detroit of Sammarinese parents and received a Ph.D. in music (saxophone performance) in 2003 from Northwestern University. He is an accomplished jazz musician, arranger, music instructor at numerous colleges and universities, has had a wide performance experience, and is involved in Catholic Church music. He is featured on several CD/DVDs as both artist/performer. His musical accomplishments are vast and varied.

Fernando Casali (1930-2006) was born in San Marino, arrived in the United States in 1954, and was known as a humble man with "hands of gold." He was a painter and sculptor who had earlier completed paintings for government buildings in San Marino. As a successful Detroit artist he worked for Titano construction.

Maria Elena D'Amelio is an internationally recognized scholar of American-Italian cinema. She had received two doctorates from the University of San Marino and State University of New York at Stony Brook. Her dissertation dealt with "Hollywood on the Tiber and Italian Cinema Practices of Transatlantic Stardom, 1949-1969." Over the years she has worked as a news editor of a TV station in San Marino to assist with the New Italian Film Festival at Lincoln Center, has taught at Stony Brook, Fordham University, and the University of the Republic of San Marino and has written extensively. In 2019 she and Giovanna Faleschini published *Italian Motherhood on Screen.*[43]

In the cultural field one dominant artist representing the Sammarinese people is Leonardo Casali, a global photographer. He was born in San Marino in 1961, moved from his home to Milan in 1986, where he developed his photographic skills at *Industria/Superstudio*. Then he moved to New York City where he remained for eleven years. His published works include fashion reportage and portraits for magazines like *Time, Newsweek, Allure, Harper's Bazaar*, and many others. Since 2005 he has been based in San Marino

Bust of San Marino at San Marino Club, Troy, Michigan.
Courtesy of author.

where he continues to work throughout the world in
exhibitions, commercial jobs, books, personal and commercial
projects related to reportage, fine art, photographs, film
documentaries, and music videos.

In connection with his Sammarinese culture his photographic essay, *"Sammarinesi," Beyond the Borders of a Small World* took him on an odyssey around the world to visit and photograph Sammarinese people. Published in 2003 with 120 photos he illustrates the various and sundry immigrants from Australia to Patagonia. It is an enlightening study, which through photos he tells the personal story of how this small nation has had a global impact.[44]

Publications

For such a small ethnic group in the United States, it is surprising that the immigrants have published a number of newspapers over the years. The first of these was *San Marino,* which was first published on September 3, 1929 in New York City. It served not only the Sammarinesi in the New York City area but those in Ohio and Detroit, Michigan. During the years of 1926 and 1936 *Il Popolo Sammarinese* was published. In later years the various social clubs produced publications as well. In 1960, the *Notiziario della Fratellanza Sammarinese, Inc.* began publication. This was a publication sent to society members in Detroit as well. The *San Marino Journal USA* whose motto is "Where unity grows stronger" was established in 1994. It is the only newspaper, written in both Italian and English, devoted to Sammarinese citizens around the world on news from San Marino, events, human-interest articles, and the latest news defending Sammarinese equal rights. It is published out of Nassau County, New York. Copies of these newspapers are available in the *Biblioteca di Stato*/State Library in San Marino. The newspaper, *The Young Sammarinesi* was first published in

87

April 1975 and was devoted to the discussion of youth activities.

Cultural Resources

Among the numerous museums and cultural resources in the Republic there are three available to the public. The Museum of the Emigrant was opened in 1997 in the old monastery of Santa Chiara. It was created as a place of remembrance, where citizens of San Marino and visitors can come to learn of the out-migration of the Sammarinesi through objects, written primary and secondary sources, oral histories, and iconographic materials.

The University of the Republic of San Marino was created in 1985 and academically reorganized in 2014. Its programs include: Department of Economics, Sciences and Law; Department of Human Science; and the Department of History and of Sammarinese culture and history. It has both undergraduate and graduate programs. A doctorate is given in historical studies, which helps to keep alive the heritage of the Republic.

The State Museum/*Museo di Stato* is an important component providing citizens of the Republic and visitors with a look into the history, heritage, and conditions of the Republic. There are also some paintings dating from the seventeenth century. The Art Museum/*Museo Pinacoteca* in the former church of San Francesco has a fine collection of paintings.

The towns surrounding the capital of San Marino are more industrialized and generally not as attractive as the main city, San Marino. The site of "San Marino and Historic Centre and Mount Titano" became part of UNESCO World Heritage Centre in 2008.

San Marino and the Movies

The Medieval-Renaissance buildings and streets of San Marino became a set for the 20th Century-Fox movie, *Prince of Foxes* with Tyrone Power and Orson Welles in 1949. A fictional story of Cesare Borgia, the 40-day shoot was filmed using San Marino's authentic setting, which cost the film company $1600. Most of the citizens served as extras in the movie. The movie is considered a visual education of the times and is the only movie made in San Marino.[45]

Immigration Monument

As we have seen there is a very close relationship between the Republic of San Marino and her immigrants around the world. Achille Maiani, a member of the Detroit Comunità, suggested the construction of the testimonial to the immigrant. His proposal was unanimously accepted and the result was the immigration monument. The circular monument split in the middle represents the Sammarinesi living in their homeland and abroad, showing that the ties are unbreakable. The monument symbolizes all the feelings of emigration: pain, homesickness, sacrifice, hope, and courage. The past, present, and future are represented by artistic expression that unites the immigrants who return to their homeland. Immigrants are proud of the monument, which represents the consideration, respect, and solidarity of the country, which is part of them wherever they live.

As Lucio Capicchioni stated at the dedication of the monument on October 1, 1986:

> The value of history, culture, traditions and labor, which every Sammarinese spreads within and outside the Republic must be appreciated and not forgotten. This marble work symbolizes all these values and is proof for all generations of the dignity and sacrifice of our people who are proud of their origins and national identity. No borders nor social status can weaken these feelings and the ties with the Sammarinese community.

Sammarinese immigration monument dedication. *Photo courtesy of author.*

San Marino, California

How did the City of San Marino get its name? The name was attached in a unique fashion. The land was originally home to Native Americans, Spanish and Mexicans in present Los Angeles County. In 1873 Benjamin "Don Benito" Wilson conveyed to his son-in-law, James DeBarth Shorb, 500 acres of old rancho land, which consisted of a large vineyard and orchards. Shorb named it "San Marino" after his grandfather's plantation in Maryland where he had spent much of his childhood. The area turned into rich agricultural land. The city was incorporated in 1913 and in 2019 had an estimated population of 13,048. The Republic of San Marino is a sister city of its California descendent

Food & Drink

Cuisine in San Marino

Surrounded by Italy it is natural that its cuisine would be similar to the cuisines of neighboring Emilia-Romagna and the Marche. Cheese, wine, and livestock are San Marino's primary agricultural products and cheese making is an important economic activity. In 1889 San Marino participated in the Exposition Universelle held in Paris with three exhibits of oils and cheese.

A number of dishes for which San Marino is famous include *fagioli con le cotiche,* a Christmas bean and bacon soup; *pasta e ceci*, a chickpea and noodle soup with garlic and rosemary; *nidi di rondine,* a baked pasta dish with smoked ham, beef, cheese, and tomato sauce; and roast rabbit with fennel. *Erbazzone* is a spinach-based dish that includes cheese and onions. There is a dish found mostly in Borgo Maggiore called a *piada*, which consists of flatbread with various fillings and is somewhat similar to a *piadina* from Emilia-Romagna.

Sweets include a layered wafer cake covered in chocolate known as *Torta Tre Monti* (Cake of the Three Mountains) based on the feature in San Marino. Another is *Torta Titano*, layered dessert made with biscuits, hazelnuts, chocolate, cream and coffee, also inspired by San Marino's mountain, Monte Titano. *Bustrengo*, a traditional Christmas cake, made with honey, nuts, and dried fruit; *Verretta*, a dessert made with milk, praline, and chocolate wafers;

Cacciatello, a dessert made with milk, sugar, and eggs similar to crème brulé; *zuppa di ciliegie* consists of cherries stewed in sweetened red wine and served on white bread.

San Marino is known for its red wines such as Brugneto and Tessano (cask-aged red wine) and Biancale and Roncale (still white wine). It also produces a sweet moscato. The San Marino Wine Association regulates the country's wine production. A number of liqueurs include: *Mistrà*, strong drink flavored with aniseed, truffle-flavored Tilus, and the herbal liqueur, Duda di Gualdo, similar to Fernet Branca.

When the immigrants came to the United States they brought with them their recipes and winemaking expertise.

Gardens and Food

Since most of the Sammarinese immigrants came from a farming background, it was natural for many of them to keep gardens in the United States. The Sammarinesi kept victory gardens in Detroit and Sandusky during World War II and even after the war many had full gardens finding space in the urban environment. During the war D. Babboni found it was fashionable to keep chickens and rabbits as did many people in Detroit. Women came home from a grueling day's working in a war-industry plant and found time to tend to their poultry and rabbits. More kept chickens since they knew what they were fed.

After the war home gardening continued even in backyard garden plots. The late summer harvest allowed Sammarinese women to can everything during the August-September harvest season. The jars were stored in basements and cellars. Meats were also stored in these areas as well. They hung sausage there, dried salamis, fresh bacon salted down and used like pancetta. This home production of food continued for many years until their children left home or they prospered and did not need to process their own food (Babboni).

At Easter lamb raised on site was the main dish for the holiday. In the Babboni household since his father refused to process the baby lamb it was his mother who took over. When done and roasted then the kids refused to eat the baby lamb!

A common and popular dish was polenta, similar to grits, but not as finely ground. Polenta, which was made into a thick porridge in the northern Alps, was made in San Marino (Uberti).

The Oakwood District was home to many Sammarinesi in the 1950s and given the semi-rural nature of the community on the edge of Detroit, large gardens were developed and this continued for many years. In the springtime the individual gardeners raced to see who produced the first vegetables of the year. Through the summer months homegrown vegetables were an important part of their diet.

Many Sammarinesi found that climatic conditions in southeastern Michigan were conducive to fruit growing. Those who moved to Rochester Hills and vicinity found they could raise fruit trees – apple, pear, cherry, plum – as this is prime fruit growing area. One immigrant decided to fight the snow and ice and sought to cultivate non-Michigan fruit trees as in his native San Marino. He had a greco olive tree and two fig trees in Rochester Hills. He carefully protected the roots from freezing and covered the small trees with visquine. He was not so much interested in getting a crop of fruit from the trees but to prove that these trees could survive Michigan's frosty winter (Ferri).

Wine & Grappa

The manufacture and use of wine goes back to the Old Country where wine has been made for thousands of years. Even in hilly San Marino there were many vineyards even placed on terraces if necessary. Making and drinking wine became an important way of life for the Sammarinesi (Amati). When the immigrants came to the United States they carried with them this important culinary tradition. As a result wine making became an important household activity within the Sammarinese community.

When the Sammarinesi arrived on Kelleys Island and vicinity they had entered the Lake Erie Grape Belt where wineries had flourished since the 1850s. Native grapes – Concord, Niagara, and Catawba – were growing out their back door. They immediately put to use their winemaking skills. They used mostly local grapes, which have a musky or foxy flavor and as a result mixed them with imported California grapes. This was also true of Sammarinese wine makers in Detroit.

There was always one winemaker in the group who was considered the "best" winemaker. They would import two hundred lugs of "perfect grapes" from California to produce their wine. At times they would go into wine partnerships with friends to facilitate the process. Usually they made two hundred gallons of wine, which would last them the year.

Sammarinesi processed grapes after the wine had been made, fermented them, added sugar to the process and made *grappa*. As a result of this distillation some Sammarinesi were able to produce *grappa* at 150-proof or 75 percent alcohol by volume. Sometimes they added a variety of anise to the *grappa* and made *mistra*. Such a potent drink is usually served in teaspoon amount in coffee. The Sammarinesi also produced home-made beer. Uberti remembered on his arrival to America living in a cold-water flat Primo Bizzocchi made beer only to have the bottle pop in the summer heat (Zanotti, Uberti, and Babboni). Boardinghouse keepers quickly learned that they could make extra money by selling wine, *grappa*, and beer at 10 cents a glass.

With the coming of national Prohibition in 1920 and the terrible economic times of the Depression of the 1930s, some Sammarinesi joined others selling their illegal alcohol. In many cases it helped them to financially survive the difficult economic times. There were lively markets for Kelleys Island *grappa* in Toledo and Cleveland. Secondo Zanotti recounted the story of a groom vanishing during the middle of his wedding reception. It seems he had to make a *grappa* delivery in Cleveland and did not let the wedding interfere (Zanotti).

Recipes

We are indebted to the San Marino Ladies Auxiliary for two cookbooks, which focus on the local cuisine.[46] The traditional meals are prepared for: New Year's Day, *Carnevale* (Tuesday prior to Ash Wednesday), Easter,

Christmas Eve and Christmas Day. The feast days of St. Marino (September 5) and St. Agatha (February 5) are times for special meals usually at the local club hall.

Some of the special Sammarinese foods are eaten during one of the above-mentioned special days. Angel Wings (*Fiochetti*), which are strips of dough tied to form a bow shape and deep-fried and served with white wine for Carnavale. On Christmas Eve following tradition there is a meal of steamed clams, roasted codfish, mixed fried fish, chickpea soup, and a variety of greens both cooked and as salads. The other holidays are celebrated with a meal of appetizers, soups, entree, vegetables, fresh fruit and dessert topped off with wine. The San Marino Women's Auxiliary of Detroit feels that "the club has grown and prospered due to its superb reputation for excellence in cuisine and service."

Picnic Lunch, typical meeting of Sammarinese prior to clubhouse construction. *Photos courtesy of author.*

Recipes:

Below follow traditional recipes from Sammarinese women:

Unleavened Bread (*Piada*)

6 c. flour	1½ Tbsp. baking powder
1 Tbsp. salt	1 c. shortening
¼ c. oil	2 ¼ c. milk

Mix all ingredients together and knead until smooth. Shape into 12 balls. Roll each ball with a rolling pin until ball is 8 inches in diameter. Cook on a hot griddle until golden brown on both sides. Poke several times with fork while cooking to prevent bubbles. Vincenza Putti

Mushrooms – Stuffed (*Funghi Ripleni*)

35 large mushrooms	3 Tbsp. olive oil
¾ c. breadcrumbs	2 hard-boiled eggs
2 Tbsp. fresh parsley	Salt and pepper to taste
2 Tbsp. butter	¾ c. grated Parmesan
2 cloves garlic	cheese

Wash mushrooms, remove stems and set caps aside. Chop mushroom stems, parsley, garlic and eggs. Mix together cheese, breadcrumbs, salt, pepper, butter, and oil. Mix all ingredients together and stuff mushroom caps with mixture. Place on buttered cookie sheet and put dab of butter on each. Bake at 350* for approximately 35 minutes. Anna Capicchioni

Fennel and Celery Salad (*Insalata di Finnocchio e Sedano*)

1 finnocchio (fennel) bulb

2 Tbsp. olive oil

4 tender celery stalks

Salt and pepper to taste

2 Tbsp. wine vinegar

Cut the fennel and celery into small chunks; wash and drain. In salad bowl, mix with all [remaining] ingredients and serve. Serves 4. Iole Francini

Passatelli Pasta in Broth (*Passatelli in Brodo*)

4 eggs

11/2 c. grated Parmesan cheese

2 Tbsp. flour

½ tsp. nutmeg

11/2 c. plain breadcrumbs

1 Tbsp. grated lemon rind

64 oz. broth (Use a basic chicken and beef broth)

Mix eggs and all dry ingredients together. Squeeze through passatelli maker or potato ricer. Drop noodles into boiling broth. Cook at gentle boil for approximately 5 minutes. Iole Francini

Roasted Pork (*Porchetta*)

6 lbs. boneless pork butt or shoulder with some skin on it

2 tsp. salt

2 Tbsp. freshly ground pepper

12 cloves chopped garlic

Significant fresh dill

Lay the shoulder out and spread salt, pepper, garlic and dill. Roll it up, enclose it with the skin, and tie it. Place in a Ziploc bag and keep in refrigerator overnight. Bake at 325* for 21/2-

31/2 hours until juices are clear. Remove roasted skin and eat on the side. Babboni & Paoletti

Rabbit Stew (*Lepre in Umido*)

1 game rabbit, sectioned
1 c. beer
1 c. vinegar (red or white)
¼ c. olive oil
2 tsp. rosemary, chopped
2-3 cloves chopped garlic
2 c. tomatoes, chopped or 1 c. tomato sauce

Soak rabbit in vinegar and water for 2 hours. Remove rabbit and cook in skillet until natural juices evaporate. Add rosemary, garlic, oil, salt, pepper, and beer. Simmer, covered, until brown, approximately ½ hour. Add tomatoes and 1-cup water. Simmer for an additional hour or until rabbit is tender. Occasionally add more water if needed. Iole Francini

Beef Marsala (*Manzo di Marsala*)

1½ lbs. fresh mushrooms thinly sliced	¼ c. Marsala wine (substitute with brandy)
¼ c. oil	6 slices beef tenderloin
2 cloves garlic, chopped	2 Tbsp. flour
2 Tbsp. chopped parsley	1 c. water
2 Tbsp. purred tomatoes	Salt and pepper to taste

Sauté mushrooms in oil and [then] water. Add parsley and garlic. Simmer until mushrooms are almost cooked. Add tomatoes and wine. Finish cooking mushrooms (more water may be added if necessary). Sprinkle salt and pepper on beef and coat with flour on both sides. Place beef in skillet with mushrooms. Cover and continue simmering to desired doneness. Daniela Crescentini

Zucchini and Shrimp (*Zucchini e Scampi*)

1/3 c. butter	¼ c. chopped fresh parsley
½ tsp. dill weed	1 Tbsp. lemon juice
2 c. sliced zucchini (about	20 medium fresh raw
¼-½ inch thick)	shrimp shelled and rinsed.
2 Tbsp. chopped onion	½ tsp. minced fresh garlic
¼ tsp. salt	Hot cooked rice

In 10-inch skillet, melt butter over medium heat. Stir in remaining ingredients, except rice. Cook over medium heat, stirring occasionally, until shrimp turns pink and zucchini is crispy tender (5 to 8 minutes). Pour sauce over hot cook rice. Serves 4. Anna Capicchioni

Angel Wings (*Fiochetti*)

3 eggs
3 c. flour
3 Tbsp. sugar

Beat eggs and sugar until fluffy. Add flour gradually until dough is the consistency of pasta. Knead dough and roll until very thin (or use pasta machine). Cut dough into strips approximately 6 inches long and 11/2 inches wide. Pinch dough in the middle to form a bow shape. Deep-fry until golden brown. Drain on paper towel to remove excess oil. Sprinkle with powdered sugar. Iole Francini

St. Joseph's "Ravioli" (*Ravioli di San Giuseppe*)

1 ¼ c. flour

Grated rind of ½ lemon

¼ c. butter

Pinch of salt

2 egg yolks

A few Tbsp. milk

3 Tbsp. jam

Mix the flour with the egg yolk, butter, lemon rind, salt and milk. Knead well, then leave the dough to rest for about 1 hour. Roll it out to a thickness of about 3/16 inch and cut three-inch large disks. Put 1 tablespoon of jam in the center of each disk, then fold the disk in half, giving it a crescent shape and seal the edges well. Butter an oven tray/ cookie sheet; place the "ravioli" on it and brush them over with some egg yolk. Bake in a medium oven at 375* F. to 400* F. for about 30 minutes. When cold, sprinkle with powdered sugar. Anna Capicchioni

Margherita Cake (*Pasta Margherita*)

11 egg yolks

2 c. sugar

3 tsp. baking powder

1 tsp. vanilla

1 c. milk, boiled & cooled

2 ½ c. cake flour

1 stick butter

Beat egg yolks with sugar until fluffy. Sift together flour and baking powder twice. Gradually add flour and milk (alternately). Add vanilla and continue beating. Fold in butter. Bake at 350* for 40 to 50 minutes. Vincenza Putti

Epilogue

The story of the Sammarinesi in the United States and Michigan in particular is unusual for a number of reasons. The first is that they are part of a micro-nation. As a result, it should be that there are too few immigrants to develop a story around them. However, they immigrated around the world. In the United States they were concentrated in Metro Detroit, Metro New York City, and Sandusky. However, it quickly became obvious that as with other ethnic groups, they spread out across the country where economic opportunity was available. Their movement followed Italian migration where they could enjoy settlement connections.

The study has delved into the details of Sammarinese immigration and finds that the first immigrants from the microstate showed up in New York in the 1870s. They landed at Clinton Castle and Ellis Island. This migration came in a series of waves. The first, starting in the 1870s lasted until World War I. The second was stimulated by the rise of fascism in the 1920s, which drove socialists and other anti-fascists from the republic through the 1930s. This political interference continued between 1945 and 1957 during the Communist domination of the country when party membership was mandatory in order to seek employment and created a third wave of immigrants. Finally immigrants continued to leave the country through the 1960s.

The Sammarinesi brought with them a love of their tiny country. This became a strong characteristic of these people and is similar to another small ethnic group –

Corsicans. The close ties with the Old Country continue with later generations. Even the earliest Sammarinese immigrants frequently returned to their former homes to visit family and friends and enjoy their hilly nation. Over the decades other immigrants returned to retire.

Finally, the Sammarinesi engaged in a series of occupations and activities. Since quarrying was an important occupation from the time of St. Marino, many Sammarinesi arrived in the United States and got into stone quarrying and into the many aspects of the construction industry. They moved from simple laborers and some developed major construction companies and built homes in the suburbs. Others developed sports activities – bobsledding, auto racing, ice-yacht racing, fishing, and hunting. The professions are filled with teachers, physicians, pharmacists, and businessmen. Others from the beginning went into the restaurant business. In field of culture Sammarinese were involved with music.

This small nation brought to the United States a small number of Sammarinesi but they played a role in the development of America.

The Sammarinese descendants continue to carry on the traditions of their fathers and grandfathers. This is seen in the San Marino Construction Company of Hempstead, Nassau County on Long Island. To the west in Howell, Michigan, San Marino Excavating does commercial and residential work, trucking and septic jobs. In the late 1980s Robert Casadei developed Casadei Development/Casadei Homes located in Auburn Hills, Michigan. In December 2001 Robert and Bruno Casadei started Casadei Steel, headquartered in Sterling Heights, which has developed as one of the biggest fabricators in the state of Michigan. It deals in all aspects of steel construction. The San Marino Italian Restaurant on Charlton Street in New York City serves Insalata Sammarinese, Fettuccini Sammarinese, and Pollo Sammarinese.

Resources in the United States & San Marino

The Bentley Historical Library, University of Michigan, 1150 Beal Ave., Ann Arbor, MI 48109-3482; PH. 734/764-3482; FAX 734/936-1333; www.umich.edu/~bhl/. Resources: interviews with Sammarinesi from Michigan, Ohio and New York; collection includes books, paper materials and photographs.

The Burton Historical Collection, Detroit Public Library, 5201 Woodward Ave., Detroit, MI 48202; PH. 313/833-1486; detroit.lib.mi.us/burton/index.htm. Resources: newspaper clippings, photographs and obituaries.

Elmont Memorial Library. 700 Hempstead Tpke, Elmont, NY 11003. 151-635-4528. Elmont and vicinity is home to many Sammarinese-American information about their settlement can be found.

Libertas Repubblica di San Marino. See: Libertas.sm. Written in Italian it can be translated on-line. It provides news, weather and information on San Marino and Romagna.

Museo dell'Emigrante - Centro Studi Permante sull'Emigrazione. Antico Monastario di Santa Chiara. Contrada Omerelli, 24; 47890 San Marino - Republic of San Marino. Telephone: (+378)05498885171; Fax 0549885170.
Resources: all material is in Italian; collection of documents, correspondence, oral interviews, and

photographs focusing on Sammarinesi throughout the world.

Queens Historical Society. 143-145 37th Avenue, Queens, NY 11354. Research and inquires by appointment only. 9:30-4:00 M-F.

San Marino Journal USA. Nassau County, New York. Rsmusajournal@aol.com; 631-242-2212 or 576-437-4699. This is the only Italian and English journal devoted to Sammarinese citizens around the world presenting news from San Marino, events, human-interest articles, and a discussion of equal rights.

San Marino Social Club, 1685 East Big Beaver Road, Troy, Michigan 48083; (museum open MWF 9:00a.m.-4:30 p.m.)
Resources: small ethnic museum; paper materials and photographs related to the club.

Bibliography

Bent, J. Theodore. *A Freak of Freedom, or, The Republic of San Marino*. London: Longmans, Green & Co., 1879; reprint, Bologna, Italy: Analisi Trend, 1985.

Brizi, Oreste. *Quadro storico-statistico della serenissima Repubblica di San Marino*, Firenze, Italia: Fabris, 1842.

Brown, Mary Elizabeth. *The Italians of the South Village*. New York: Greenwich Village Society for Historical Research, 2007.

Bruc, Charles de. *The Republic of San Marino*. Translated by William W. Tucker. Cambridge, Mass.: Riverside Press, 1880.

Brundenell, Mike. "Passion for Racing, Life, Rochester Hills Driver [Dino Crescentini] Excelled," *Detroit Free Press* 06-27-2008, p. 27

Capicchioni, Livio. "Origini dell'emigrazione Sammarinese negli Stati Uniti d'America," *San Marino Journal USA* (Summer 1997): 8.

---. *The Sporting Life of Fred Cappy (Fernando Capicchioni)*. Farmington Hills, MI; Privately published, 1988.

Casali, Leonard and Ferdinand Scianna. *Sammarinese: Beyond the Borders of a Small World / Oltre i confine di un piccolo mondo.* Venice, Italy: Electa, 2003.

Catling, Christopher. *Umbria, the Marches and San Marino.* New York: McGraw Hill, 1994.

Chiarelli, Renzo. *Rimini and San Marino.* Florence: Bonechi Editore, 1970.

Cinelli, Ferdinand H. "San Marinese," in James M. Anderson and Iva A. Smith, eds. The Peoples of Michigan Series. vol. 1: Ethnic Groups in Michigan. Detroit: The Michigan Ethnic Heritage Studies Center and the University of Michigan Ethnic Studies Program, 1983, pp. 235-37.

Cosí Lontano, Cosí Vicini: l'emigrazione sammarinese tra storia e memoria. San Marino: Ufficio del Lavoro, 1996.

Dall'Olmo, Carlo Augusto. "A Nine Day Voyage to A Six Decade Journey," [2009], deposited at the Bentley Library, University of Michigan, Ann Arbor.

Dilanian, Ken. "Tiny Nation, Good Economy," *Detroit Free Press,* 07/25/2003, 10A:1.

Duursma, Jorri. *Fragmentation and the International Relations of Micro-States: Self-Determination and Statehood.* (Cambridge Studies in International and

Comparative I). New York: Cambridge University Press, 1996.

Eccardt, Thomas M. *Secrets of the Seven Smallest States of Europe: Andorra, Liechenstein, Luxembourg, Malta, Monaco, San Marino, and Vatican City.* New York: Hippocrene Books, 2007.

Edwards, Adrian and Chris Michaelides. *San Marino.* vol. 188, World Bibliographical Series. Santa Barbara, CA: Clio Press, 1996.

Epstein, Reid J. "In Elmont Home Tiny Republic Consul Reigns," *Newsday* (Long Island/Nassau), 06-24-2009.

Felici, Monica, Adele Berardi, and Maria R. Miccioli, compilers. *Rielaborazione grafica di alcuni dati statistici sul fenomeno dell'emigrazione Sammarinese.* [Graphic Revision of Some Statistical Data Concerning the Phenomenon of Sammarinese Immigration] San Marino: Segreteria di Stato per Gli Affari Esteri, 1995.

Gasparoni, Marina, editor. *A Small State in the Great History: San Marino Emigration between Event and Narration.* Ellis Island Immigration Museum, 21st April - 28th May 2001. [New York: Ellis Island Immigration Museum, 2001.

Gasperoni, Michaël. *La Communauté juive de la République de Saint-Marin, XVIe-XVIIe siècles.* Paris: Éditions Publibook Université, 2011.

---. *Poplazione, famiglie e parentela nella Repubblica di San Marino in età moderna.* Collana Sammarinese di Studi Storici, n. 28, Universita di San Marino, 2009.

Gentileschi, Maria Luisa. "Immigration to Italy and Return Policies: A Provocation, A Wishful Thinking or an Opportunity?" *Documents d'anàlisi geografica* Vol. 53 (2009): 11-28.

Grady, Ellen. *Blue Guide: The Marche and San Marino.* 2nd edition. London: Blue Guide, 2015.

Guardigli, P. P. "L'emigrazione," *Storia illustrate della Repubblica di San Marino.* Vol. 2. San Marino: AIEP, 1985.

Harris, Credo. "San Marino, The Smallest of the Allies," *New Outlook* vol. 111 (October 27, 1915): 503-509.

Hillinger, Charles. "The Cinderella Republic of San Marino," *Toledo Magazine, The Blade* 02-05-1978: 5-8.

Kaufman, Michelle. "Tiny Hope, San Marino's Glory: Our Novice Sledders," *Detroit Free Press* 11-20-1993.

King, R. J. "Three Towers," *DBusiness* 12-26-2014.

La Gumina, Salvatore. *From Steerage to Suburb: Long Island Italians.* New York: Center for Migration Studies, 1988.

Lambert, G. "The Republic of San Marino," *The Month and Catholic Review.* Vol. 26 (March 1876): 277-96.

Magnaghi, Russell M. "Italian Railroad Laborers on the Northern Plains," manuscript. (2000).

Matteini, Nevio. *The Republic of San Marino: Historic and Artistic Guide.* Translated by Shirley O'Gorman and Verdiana Medri. San Marino: Azienda Tipografia Edutoriale, 1981.

Miller, William. "The Republic of San Marino," *American Historical Review* 6:4 (July 1901): 633-49.

Montalbo, Luigi, Amedée Astraudo and Amedeo Galatti di Riella. *Dizionario Bibliografico Iconografico della Repubblica di San Marino.* Parigi, Francia: Protat Frères Imprimeurs, 1898.

Newspapers:
Detroit Free Press
Detroit News
Great Falls Tribune (Great Falls, Montana)
New York Times
The Missoulian (Missoula, Montana)
Ravalli Republic (Hamilton, Montana)

Pedrocco, Giorgio. *L'emigrazione nella storia sammarinese tra Ottocento e Novocento.* San Marino: Edizioni del Titano, 1998.

Rail, Evan. "Seeking Authenticity in Italy's Tiny Neighbor," *New York Times,* "Travel," 11-22-2013.

Rogatnick, Joseph H. "Little States in a World of Powers: A Study of Conduct of Foreign Affairs by Andorra, Lichtenstein, Monaco, and San Marino," Ph.D. dissertation, University of Pennsylvania, 1976.

Rohe, Alice. "Our Littlest Ally," *National Geographic Magazine* 34 (August 1918): 139-63.

Rossi, Giuseppe. *San Marino: Historical and Artistic Itinerary*. San Marino: Studiostampa, S.A., [c.2000].

St. Hippolyte, Auger. *The Republic of San Marino*. Trans. William W. Tucker. Cambridge, MA: Riverside Press, 1880. First published in 1827.

"San Marino," in *Western Europe, 2003*. 5th edition. London & New York: Europa Publications, 2003, pp. 553-58.

San Marino Ladies Auxiliary. *La Cucina di San Marino: Recipes of the San Marino Ladies Auxiliary*. Troy, MI: San Marino Ladies Auxiliary, 1994.

"San Marino Social Club: A Legacy Kept to Be Maintained," *Libertas* (May 22, 2006).

San Marino Social Club: Statuto/By-Laws. (Revised November 2000). [Troy, MI: San Marino Social Club, 2001.]

San Marino Social Club, Troy, Michigan, 1938-1988. Troy: San Marino Social Club, 1988.

Schatzer, P. "Changing Patterns of Migration in the Adriatic Region," *International Migration* (Geneve) 26:2 (1988): 215-19.

Secretary of State for Foreign Affairs. *Immagini Memoria Coscienza: Il Bombardamento del 26 giugno 1944.* Repubblica di San Marino: Segreteria di Stato, 1996. (Photos of 1944 bombing).

Shrayer, Maxim D. "Napoleon at San Marino," *Southwest Review* 92:2 (2007): 215-234.

Shutt, David. "San Marino on Their Minds," *Toledo Magazine, The Blade*, 02/05/1978, 4-5.

Stiles, Kendall W. *Trust and Hedging in International Relations.* Ann Arbor: The University of Michigan Press, 2018.

United States Department of State. *Background Notes: San Marino.* Washington, D.C.: U.S. Department of State, 1987.

Veenendaal, Wouter P. "The Economic Crisis and the Politics of the Republic of San Marino: A Comparative Case Study," Conference Paper, 6th ECPR General Conference (August 2011).

Venturini, Roberto. "Movimenti consuetudinari, mobilità, emigrazione europea e transoceanica nei documenti di espatrio sammarinesi tra Otto e Novecento," *Studi emigrazione* 138 (2000): 405-429.

---. *Dopo nove giorni di cielo e acqua. Storia, storie e luoghi in mezzo secolo di emigrazione sammarinese negli Stati Uniti.* Repubblica di San Marino: Edizioni del Titano, 1999.

---. "Terre straniere. L'emigrazione sammarinese negli Stati Uniti, 1920–1970." Tesi di laurea, Università degli Studi di Bologna, Facoltà di Lettere e Filosofia, 1996–1997.

Appendix A			
Social Conditions of Immigrants, 1923-1953			
Trades	1923	1933	1943	1953
---	---	---	---	---
Craftsmen	34	44	54	101
Day Laborers	15	10	171	21
Housewives	36	20	58	34
Laborers	16	13	29	23
Skilled Laborers	8	1	14	10
Students	0	9	43	29
Tenant Farmers	45	9	43	41
TOTAL	171	128	515	289

Appendix B:
Number of Passports Issued to Sammarinesi Between 1923 and 1962

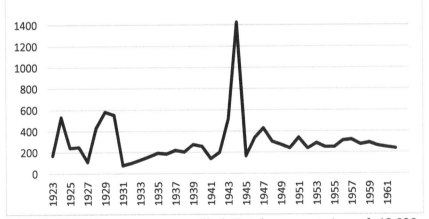

Missing data: 3 passports cancelled. Total passports issued: 12,030.

Appendix C Emigration Nations Relative to the Years:				
Nations	**1927/29**	**1937/39**	**1947/49**	**1957/59**
Argentina	22	2	31	0
France	831	150	334	258
Italy	53	339	380	71
Other	22	167	164	347
Switzerland	18	6	32	21
United States	179	33	125	195
TOTAL	1,125	697	1,006	892

Appendix D
Occupations Employing Sammarinese Immigrants
in the Twentieth Century

Accountant	Ice company laborer
Amusement Park rides	Limestone quarry laborer
Auto laborer, mechanic	Machine operator, Carhart
Barber	Machinist
Beauty salon	Mason, stone
Boat builder	Mechanic
Bobsledder	Merchant
Businessman	Molder, Iron
Cabinet maker	Nurse
Carpenter	Physician
Chemical plant fireman	Pipe mill laborer
Cement contractor	Railroad laborer, car repairman, section hand
Cement work (flat)	Real estate developer
Clerk	Restaurateur
Construction, homes	Rubber factory laborer
Consul for Republic	Scavenger
Cook	Shipping clerk
Cycling	Shoemaker
Factory laborer	Seamstress
Farmer	Stone quarry laborer
Fireman power plant	Street & sewer construction
Fisherman	Surveyor
French fry stand	Tailor
Fruit dealer	Terrazzo worker/layer
Gasket mfr foreman	Tile, setter,
Glass company laborer	Watch company packer
Grocer	

Endnotes

[1] Thomas M. Eccardt. *Secrets of the Seven Smallest States of Europe.* New York: Hippocrene Books, 2007, pp. 277+.

[2] New York *Daily News* 09-07-1929, 04-13-1958, 06-07-1959, 04-01-1965, 02-26-1966, 05-31-1967, 10-31-1971.

[3] The honorary consuls in Detroit/Troy: Livio Capicchioni, Joseph Putti, and Alessandro Vincenti.

[4] For an overview of Sammarinese global settlement see: Leonard Casali and Ferdinand Scianna. *Sammarinese: Beyond the Borders of a Small World/Oltre i confine di un piccolo mondo.* Venice, Italy: Electa, 2003.

[5] 1930 Federal Census, New York, Westchester County, Tuckahoe, District 0124, p. 48, and Monica Felici, Adele Berardi, and Maria R. Micciolo, compilers. *Rielaborazione grafica di alcuni dati statistici sul fenomeno dell'emigrazione sammarinese.* San Marino: Secreteria di Stato per gli Affari Esteri, 1995, p. 2.

[6] P. P. Guardigli. "L'emigrazione," *Storia illustrate della Repubblica di San Marino.* Vol. 2. San Marino: AIEP, 1985.

[7] U.S. Naturalization Records, 1791-1992, County Court, Richmond County, New York, vol. 4, p. 3; New York, State and Federal Naturalization Records, 1794-1946.

[8] Federal Census, New York, New York City, 1900-1930, under Giovanni Renganeschi.

[9] Based on Federal census, New York, New York City, 1910-1940.

[10] Federal Census, New York, New York City, 1910-1940 under the Lombardi family: Giovanni, Eugenia, Bruno, Julius, Santora, Hamlet, George (Kino); New York Passenger Lists, 1820-1957, Eugenia Lombardi.

[11] Luigi Lombardi. New York Passenger Lists, 1820-1957, Roll T715, 1897-1957, Reel 3857.

[12] Marie A. Giannini-Raptis, "La Familia Giannini Est. 1951, New York City," *San Marino Journal USA* (Summer 1997), 12.

[13] Salvatore J. Gumina. *From Steerage to Suburb: Long Island Italians.* New York: Center for Migration Studies, 1988.

[14] Richard Panczyk. *A History of Westbury, Long Island.* Charleston, SC: Arcadia Publishing Company, 2007, pp 14 and 40

[15] 1930 Federal Census, New York, Westchester County, Tuckahoe, District 0124, p. 48.

[16] 1930 Federal Census, New Jersey, Monmouth County, Marlboro, District 0151, pp. 2-3.

[17] US Passenger and Crew List, New York, 1926 May 12, p.185; 1920 US Census, New York, Niagara County, Niagara Falls Ward 4, District 0105, p. 115; Capicchioni Interview.

[18] *Convegno emigrazione sammarinese* (1987), p. 54.

[19] Luigi Ceccoli first worked at the foundry and became a foreman. Soon after he sent for his nephew, Secondo Zanotti and when he arrived from San Marino, Luigi immediately had him hired. Unfortunately, Secondo only lasted twelve days on the job. He suffered from asthma and could not handle the smoky environment. His other uncle John Ceccoli was in construction work and hired Secondo who was trained as a bricklayer, retiring in 1990.

[20] Arthur Amati and Joseph Putti interviews. (All interviews are at Bentley Library University of Michigan, Ann Arbor.)

[21] Joseph Putti Interview.

[22] *Detroit Free Press* 05-18-1941, 04-26-1942, 01-03-1943,10-31-1943, 02-21-1943, 01-02-1944, 05-27-1956,

[23] *Detroit Free Press* 10-24-1998.

[24] Dino Crescentini interview; Mike Brundenell. "Passion for Racing, Life, Rochester Hills Driver," *Detroit Free Press* 06-27-2008.

[25] Joseph Putti interview.

[26] United States, New York, Arriving Passenger and Crew Lists, New York, "Bugli," 1914 March 24, p. 157. 1920 Federal Census, Montana, Missoula County, Missoula, District 0151, pp 2-3; *Great Falls Tribune* 07-01-1926.

[27] *Missoulian* Missoula, Mont. 01-27-1964, 06-12-1985, 11-30-1985.

[28] For specific news stories about members of the Bugli family check the on-line newspaper index for the following newspapers: *Great Fall Tribune* (Great Falls, Mont.) *Missoulian* Missoula, Mont. and *Ravalli Republic* (Hamilton, Mont.).

[29] U.S. Passenger and Crew List, New York, 1922 September 8, p. 157; 1930 Federal Census, California, Siskiyou County, Edgewood, District 0037, p. 14; 1940 Federal Census, California, Siskiyou County, Edgewood, District 47-6, p. 35.

[30] U.S. Passenger and Crew List, New York, 1924 August 17, p. 68;1930 Federal Census, California, Siskiyou County, Mott, District 0022, p. 10; 2930 Census, California, Siskiyou County, Edgewood, District 0037, p. 50.

[31] Without burdening the reader with all of the figures the 1939 price of $450 would be comparable to $8,158 in 2018 and $1,600 valued at $29,007 in 2018.

[32] *Brooklyn Daily Eagle* 06-21-1941, 07-06-1941, interview with Roberto Balsimelli 2018.

[33] *News Herald* (Port Clinton, Ohio) 05-02 and 05-03-2007.

[34] *Sandusky Register* 07-28-1964, p. 16; 12-27-1995, p. 1; 01-13-2002, p. 2; 05-23-2002, p. 6.

[35] *Missoulian* 12-08-1943, 02-14-1947, 06-13-1950; *Ravalli Republic* 03-12-1942, 01-06-1944, 0711-06-12-1950, 07-14-1950.

[36] Sandusky *Morning Journal* 07-21-2006.

[37] Livio Capicchioni. *The Sporting Life of Fred Cappy* (Fernando Capicchioni). Farmington Hills, Mich.; Privately published, 1988. This invaluable publication is filled with news clippings from Cappy's career.

[38] *Detroit News* 01-13-2018.

[39] Mike Brudenell. "Passion for Racing, Life," *Detroit Free Press* 06-27-2008.

[40] W. Babboni Interview.

[41] W. Babboni and Giancarlo Ferri Interview.

[42] *San Marino Journal USA* (Summer 2004), p. 8.

[43] "Stony Brook Recognizes Maria Elena D'Amelio," *San Marino Journal USA* (March 2013), p. 13.

[44] Leonardo Casali with introduction by Fernando Scianna. *"Sammarinesi," Beyond the Borders of a Small World*. Milan, Italy: Electa Mondardori, 2003.

[45] *Brooklyn Daily Eagle* 12-18-1949, 01-17-1950.

[46] San Marino Ladies Auxiliary. *La Cucina di San Marino: Recipes of the San Marino Ladies Auxiliary*. Troy, MI: San Marino Ladies Auxiliary, 1994 is an excellent source for Sammarinese cuisine. It is available through the auxiliary, and a copy has been deposited at the Bentley Library.